Leading Ladies

Transformative
Biblical Images
for Women's
Leadership

by Jeanne Porter, Ph.D.

Innisfree Press, Inc.
Philadelphia, PA

Published by Innisfree Press, Inc.
136 Roumfort Road
Philadelphia, PA 19119
Visit our website at www.InnisfreePress.com

Cover art by Cathaleen B. Rich, 221 South Wesley, Oak Park, IL
60302. Her cards can be found at www.liminaorg.com.

Cover design by Hugh Duffy, PhD Design, Carneys Point, NJ

Library of Congress Cataloging-in-Publication Data
Porter, Jeanne, (date)
    Leading Ladies : transformative biblical images for women's leadership / by Jeanne Porter.
        p. cm.
    Includes bibliographical references.
    ISBN 1-880913-45-3
    1. Leadership—Biblical teaching. 2. Women—Biblical teaching.
3. Christian leadership. 4. Women in church work.
5. Bible, O.T.—Criticism, interpretation, etc.   I. Title.
BS1199.L4 P67 2000
262'.1'082—dc21   00-058061

To the memory of my Granny—Nellie VanLier.

Then Paul, as his custom was, went in to them,
and for three Sabbaths reasoned with them from the Scriptures
explaining and demonstrating that the Christ had to suffer
and rise again from the dead, and saying,
"This Jesus whom I preach to you is the Christ."
And some of them were persuaded;
and a great multitude of devout Greeks,
and not a few of the leading [ladies]
joined Paul and Silas.

—Acts 17:1ff-4, author's paraphrase

Contents

THE LEADER AS CHOREOGRAPHER

THE LEADER AS WEAVER

THE LEADER AS INTERCESSOR

Acknowledgments

It takes faith and the support and encouragement of family and friends to complete a project of this magnitude. I thank God for hovering over me and helping me see Puah, Shiphrah, Miriam, Deborah, and Esther in a new light.

What has become the book *Leading Ladies* was first conceived as a course for women in the Sunday Morning Bible Study (SMBS) curriculum at my church, the Apostolic Church of God in Chicago. The Director of SMBS, Rosa Sailes, had encouraged me to develop an elective course for women that related to my area of interest. In graduate school, I focused on leadership and gender studies, and I felt led to combine the issues for this course. Those first few years were so rewarding as we grappled with issues of leadership styles and development for women from a biblical perspective. There are a number of women from those early courses who have grown and become even more dynamic leaders. I will always retain a debt of gratitude to Bishop Arthur Brazier, pastor of the Apostolic Church of God, for creating a theological and ministerial space of grace in which we as members and ministers can be free to be all God has called us to be. *Leading Ladies* is an integral part of my calling.

A seminar series proved to be the next format for teaching spiritual principles of leadership for women, and we held the first series of seminars in Chicago. I am grateful to the team of women who caught the vision and helped me to sponsor, plan, and host those first Leading Ladies seminars—Yolanda Peppers, Helen Crawley, Barbara Evans, Bernadine Jackson-Kelly, Colette Luckie, Sharon Monteaux, Michelle Ross, Lee Riley, Kay Robinson, LaShaunn Tappler, and Yolanda Williams. I give special thanks to Wanda Jackson for reading every word of the manuscript and offering her insightful suggestions and expertise to this project.

I am grateful to my circle of "sister ministers" who provided prayer support, counsel, and encouragement through the birthing of this book—Dr. Chandra Taylor Smith, Dr. Brenda Salter-McNeil, Dr. Carolyn Showell, Dr. Sandra Smith, and Evang. Adair Washington. I am especially grateful to Marcia Broucek for seeing the potential of this book from the very beginning, for inviting me to join the Innisfree publishing family, and then for skillfully bringing the idea to market—she is truly a weaver.

Finally, to all the contemporary leading ladies who shared their stories for this book—Gina, Nancy Abernathy, Evang. Ann Storey Pratt, Brenda, Thea Ward, Debra J. Collins, Helen Crawley, Margaret Birt, Rev. Willie Barrow, Prya, and Maria—thank you for leading the way for a new generation of leaders.

Introduction

Women have always been leaders. Yet when I began studying leadership, I discovered very few books on the subject of women's leadership. Now, more than ever, as women accept the call to leadership in the new millennium, we need new images and models that embody women's unique styles of leading.

In *Leading Ladies* I present the stories of five Old Testament women who were leaders in their own right. Although these women have been with us for ages, they have not, until recently, been noted as leaders or profiled as role models.[1] Now, as our understanding of leadership has evolved, we can examine their stories through a different lens. The distinct leadership styles of these courageous and skillful women point us toward new images of leadership: ways of talking about and seeing leadership that honor women's experiences and perspectives.

These women of antiquity—Puah and Shiphrah, Miriam, Deborah, and Esther—all held formal positions of leadership in their day. While a major part of *Leading Ladies'* premise is that many women are leaders *whether they are named as leaders or not*, I started with women who did hold recognized leadership positions, to explicitly show the presence of female leaders in the Bible—even when limited to traditional positions. There is evidence within the text, and from other extant sources, that these women fit the prevailing notions of leadership of their time. They were also leaders by virtue of what they did and the results they achieved.

To these ancient stories I have added the voices of contemporary women who lead in their footsteps. My goal is to uncover the lessons of leadership that emerge from these "female role models"[2] and to present four images of leadership that are relevant to contemporary women: the leader as MIDWIFE, the leader as CHOREOGRAPHER, the leader as WEAVER, and the leader as INTERCESSOR. Some of these images are newer to our leadership litany; some are expanded images that are given new life by the stories of these women of antiquity:

- The leader as MIDWIFE helps give birth to ideas and dreams, developing and nurturing people to realize their God-given potential. The Egyptian midwives Puah and Shiphrah had risen to top positions of authority, overseeing a sizable organization of other midwives. They speak to us about birthing generations and remind us of the midwifing function of the leader to birth new leaders and new ideas.[3]

- The leader as CHOREOGRAPHER transforms the independent dance of individuals into the graceful, synchronized movement of collective purpose. The story of Miriam the prophetess, sister of Moses and co-leader of the leadership team that brought people out of slavery in Egypt, encourages us to dance and celebrate.[4]

- The leader as WEAVER sees beyond the present reality and braids the fibers of a hopeful future. She brings together the right people, knitting the relationships that unite and strengthen the group, giving them reason and means to work together for a better alternative. Deborah the judge demonstrates the importance of relationship to leadership and shows us how to weave together relational patterns for better outcomes.[5]

■ The leader as INTERCESSOR is strategically placed to influence the lives of others. She facilitates the liberation of a group of people by telling the story of those who have no voice or who are not in place to tell their own story. Esther, in marrying the King of Persia, became the Queen of Persia, a position of power and influence in the Persian kingdom. Her story reminds us of the importance of leaders who are in strategic places to speak for those who cannot speak for themselves.

The stories of the contemporary women mirror these images of leader as midwife, choreographer, weaver, and intercessor. You will find few "famous" women in these pages because I believe that lessons on leadership can be learned from females leaders all around us, walking different paths, in different ways. The women I describe lead in a variety of contexts—some are prominent in education, some run their own businesses, some are active in civic and community groups, and others influence churches and faith-based organizations. All the women featured in this book are women who were faced with great challenges and who followed God's call to change situations and lives.

Each leadership image presents an aspect of what I define as transformative leadership[6]—the movement of people toward collective and mutual goals of spiritual growth, higher purpose, and empowerment.

Transformative leadership is about freeing people to be who God called them to be and enabling them to lead according to their God-given gifts. Transformative leaders are visionary—they can see what others cannot, or do not, see. Transformative leaders move people to places and accomplishments they dared not go or do on their own. The midwife leader sees the potential in people and helps to birth new leaders. The choreographer envisions ideals and makes them tangible for others to see. The weaver brings a vision to life by interconnecting strategies and people. The intercessor envisions changed conditions in which dispossessed people can become empowered.

As more and more women today are accepting the challenge of leadership, more and more women are looking for resources and tools that speak to their experiences. *Leading Ladies* can be used as a personal resource to read and reflect upon the lessons on leadership, and as a book for group study and discussion. Each chapter includes a set of questions to deepen your reflection and discussion.

As leaders, God gifts each of us differently. We will be the best leaders we can be when we accept God's gifting and stop trying to lead like someone else. May *Leading Ladies* be a tool that helps you to gain insight into your own distinct ways of leading and transforming lives, and may the stories and lessons inspire you to lead in the ways God has uniquely gifted you.

Chapter 1

Women Have Always Led

My maternal grandmother was the pastor of a small Pentecostal church in the rolling hills of western Pennsylvania. As a child, I grew up seeing her minister to and lead a small vibrant congregation. Granny was not an anomaly to me. Along with my father who was a community leader, I now realize she was one of the earliest examples of a leader that I saw firsthand. I heard that my father had led civil-rights protest marches in our small town, like those being staged across the country in the 1960s, but I was very young so I never actually saw him lead the community. But every Sunday I did see my grandmother lead our congregation in worship from the pulpit of our church.

Her down-home singing was passionate and her Bible preaching fiery. Granny was revered and respected by the members of the church, as well as by the larger community, and everyone called her "Mother VanLier." I was twelve years old when she died, and the community rallied around our large extended church family to support us in our time of grieving. The packed church nestled atop the hillside of Ohio Avenue was fitting tribute to the indelible mark she left upon the community.

For many of us—women and men—our lives reflect the presence and influence of women leaders. When I was preparing to teach my first course on women and leadership at my church, a colleague who was an assistant pastor of the church reinforced my basic premise with these encouraging words: "Jeanne, make sure you teach that women have always led." This young man, a leader in his own right, was the son of one of the most powerful leaders in Chicago. He was intimately acquainted with the power of women leaders because he worked with women leaders, studied women in leadership and, like my own grandmother, his clergy grandmother made a lasting impact on his life.

Even in our churches that may not be as sensitive to acknowledging or accepting women in preaching ministries, there have always been "Church Mothers"[1] who wielded influence and power in the traditional churches of the African American community (and I suspect in many other faith traditions as well). These women may not have been labeled "leaders" but they did lead the church— sometimes from the pew, sometimes from the prayer room, sometimes from the kitchens of our churches. Yes, we have had a long tradition of experiencing women in leadership. These early leading ladies did not usurp men's authority, nor did they usurp the authority of other women. They simply followed the "leading of the Lord" by working together for the building and strengthening of God's people.

The ambiguity of who is named a leader, and who is not, raises some specific and special issues for women in leadership positions. Until recently, women (especially women of color) have not been included in the predominant leadership conversation; women have been left out of the formal definitions by the scholars who study leadership. In traditional leadership studies, women have not been the models for discussion. Consequently the voices, the patterns, and the styles of women leaders have often been overlooked. So, a woman who might project the same behaviors and perform the same actions as a man might not be called the leader. Several studies on leadership document that a woman who may have performed as a leader was more prone to call herself a "coordinator" than an actual leader.[2] Perhaps these women were hesitant to use the label for themselves because their images of "leader" had been reserved for executives, generals, or someone else at the top who had always been a man.

Another issue that surfaces for women in leadership is that the way we influence or lead may not resemble the traditional models of leadership. Some writers suggest that women are more collaborative, that they seek more input from followers, or that they partner more with co-laborers than men, and these styles are usually not recognized as qualities of leadership. Scholars of leadership are now calling for a shift to more collaborative, collective, or consultative leadership models, but prior to the mid-1990s these models were not popular, even though they may have been more consistent with female ways of leading.[3]

We are in great need of models for leadership that include women who lead in a wide variety of styles. We have grown beyond the boundaries of traditional gender-prescribed leadership roles. It is time for a new definition of leadership, for transformative leadership that is liberating—for both women and men.

Valuing Difference

Traditional leadership models tend to encourage women to assimilate male models. Think back to the workplace of the 1980s when many women were just beginning to enter into management ranks and influential corporate and government positions in large numbers. We worked hard to fit in. In those days, "fitting in" meant not making waves, not rocking the boat. Fitting in meant suppressing many so-called "female" characteristics, such as being emotional and wearing "feminine" dresses. I watched the women above me who were in positions of authority and responsibility in the corporate ranks wearing very structured blue or gray suits, white starched shirts (could they be called blouses even?), accessorized with perky silk bows tied at the collar. The fashion industry colluded in this masquerade. In their best-selling books, dress-for-success writers instructed women how to succeed in corporate America: They encouraged women to dress like men in "corporate drag."

Women assimilated the male leadership model in other ways as well. A woman dared not show empathy or compassion, lest she be labeled as soft or perceived as unable to "cut it" in the management ranks. She certainly was not supposed to cry. Though men could display plenty of emotions—including anger, aggression, and frustration by screaming in meetings and banging on desks—crying was a taboo emotion with a pejorative label and associated with women. No, emotion did not belong in the workplace . . . at least not *women's* emotions.

I remember the first time a woman cried in a meeting I attended. After the meeting, I confronted her in the ladies' room saying, "Don't you ever do that again! How dare you cry in this workplace?" I thought her tears were aimed at manipulating the men in the meeting. I never even considered that she was expressing genuine emotion. I had bought into the myth—hook, line, and sinker. I had assimilated to the male model and mold.

Fortunately, our workplaces have changed significantly from those earlier places of commerce, but there are still residual, yet subtle, misconceptions about what it means to be a woman and a leader, especially in the still male-dominated fields. Recently, I conducted a high-level executive training session for a group of company leaders who were responsible for setting direction and helping to create a high-performing organization.

The president and marketing vice-president were women, while the other executive staff members present were all men of varying ages and backgrounds.

In a conversation about valuing difference, I commented that I felt it was a shame when people dipped me into the mythical melting pot of homogeneity rather than recognizing the valuable perspective I brought to the table as an African American woman. "These naysayers insist they don't see me as a black woman," I continued. "For a person *not* to see me as a black woman is to ignore a very evident part of my identity. This so-called colorblindness suggests the person either has a set of stereotypic notions of what it means to be a black woman—and I don't fit their defined label—or the person is attempting to minimize any differences in the name of meritocracy or superficial equality."

The female executives of this company commented in some form, "But I'm not insulted when men make a similar comment to me." The marketing executive argued, "When a man tells me, 'I don't see you as a woman,' that lets me know men have accepted me and that I can compete with them."

Unfortunately, the attempt to ignore differences along gender lines tends to occur most often in arenas that previously have been male-dominated and defined. Capable, qualified women work hard to rise to the ranks of their leadership only to be told, "I don't see you as a woman." What these women are really being told, I believe, is, "You don't fit the idea of 'woman' that I have in my head. In many ways you are much like me. And the aspects where we differ surely have no bearing on your ability to lead. In fact, I can ignore those ways in which you differ from me." Unfortunately, rather than signal the arrival of women into the leadership ranks as equal and capable colleagues on their own terms, gender-blind comments such as this belie a subtle stereotyping of what it means to be woman and leader. Perhaps these comments reveal an unconscious desire to strip the leader of her womanness. They certainly ignore the unique perspective that the woman leader brings to the conversation specifically because she *is* a woman.

Ironically, this forced gender assimilation works another way. I now hear men confessing that they never were comfortable with many of the assumptions of traditional leadership, which forced them to fit a mythic image, prevented them from showing compassion, blocked their collaboration with peers or employees, or left them little time to balance their family lives. Both men and women have spent an inordinate amount of energy playing the leadership game instead of truly leading from their inner strengths.

New Bottles for New Wine

Leadership is a cultural practice, a phenomenon deeply ingrained and widely accepted in most societies. While most of the world believes in the role of leaders and leadership, there are differences in what each culture means by the term and a wide variety of ways in which leadership is recognized. How leadership gets talked about in corporations, in the media, in schools, around the kitchen table, and in churches reinforces the models of leadership that are acceptable. Our *images* of leadership usually define our concept of leadership.

Close your eyes for a moment and imagine your idea of a leader. Whom or what do you see? In the business and communication courses I teach, I usually introduce the segment on leadership by asking students to develop a list of leaders. The point of the listing is not to identify specific leadership traits, but to note who counts as leaders in their minds. In my early days of teaching, invariably the list would include Abraham Lincoln, George Washington, Adolph Hitler, and a number of other public male figures. Over the years, the lists grew to include Dr. Martin Luther King Jr., Malcolm X, Gandhi, and Cesar Chavez. As our culture's understanding of leadership changed, and women joined men as icons of leadership, the lists expanded to include Mother Teresa, Harriet Tubman, and Susan B. Anthony.

I like to think of the concept of leadership as a rich wine representing our multifaceted cultural understanding of what it means to lead and who counts as leader. As the wine ages, the more it appeals to connoisseurs. As our understanding of leadership matures, the more it appeals to and represents the actions of a broad base of people—women and men. Our images, language, and metaphors, on the other hand, are like the bottles or wineskins that hold the wine. They are the carriers of our ideas, or ideals, reinforcing the accepted parameters of leadership.

Jesus talked about the folly of putting new wine in old wineskins (Matthew 9:17), cautioning that the ferment of the new wine would cause the already stretched skins to burst. New wine had to be placed in new wineskins that could absorb the fermenting wine and stretch accordingly. So it is with our new and expanded understanding of leadership—it must be placed in new carriers, for the old carriers of leadership have been stretched to their limits. The wine is fermenting and the skins are bursting. It is time to examine the carriers carefully to make sure they adequately convey the richness of the substance they contain.

The Images of Leadership

Our images of leader provide evidence of how we implicitly define leadership and whom we unconsciously consider to be leaders. Some people envision a tall, authoritative male image, a composite of all the presidents of the United States. Clearly women such as Shirley Chisolm, Elizabeth Dole, and others have had to battle this "presidential image" embedded within the collective unconsciousness of the citizens of the United States.[4]

When picturing a leader, some people have an image of a military commander, perhaps a fully decorated and stoic Napoleon, fearlessly positioned at the bow of a boat with one hand firmly gripping the sword at his side and the other nestled inside the front opening of his overcoat, standing boldly, with resolve and conviction of certain victory in his eyes.

Others may picture an adroit, fully armored quarterback who, with ten minutes remaining in the championship game, emerges from a huddle with ten other similarly clad men and makes a daring play to bring his underdog team out from behind. The crowd rises—and then a hush descends. In one graceful sweeping motion, the heroic quarterback executes a strategically magical pass that seems to float into the arms of the open wide receiver.

When thinking "leader," few people picture a middle-aged woman quietly persuading people, shaping policy, and taking personal responsibility for the outcome—yet these are what world leaders such as Indira Gandhi, Margaret Thatcher, and Golda Meir did.

When thinking "leader," few people envision a five-foot-something blond woman leading the biggest (at that time) Initial Public Offering in United States history. Yet that picture describes Carly Fiorina, the former group president of Lucent Technologies and one of only a handful of women who lead a Fortune 500 company. A friend of mine within Lucent, who observed Ms. Fiorina's rise to the top, describes her not only as impressive and dynamic but also as a woman who maintains a stylish female touch.[5] In 1999 Ms. Fiorina became CEO of Hewlett Packard, the first woman CEO of one of America's twenty largest corporations.[6]

When picturing a leader, few people have in mind a four-foot-eleven dynamo with a large voice and compelling ideas. Yet that is an accurate image of Reverend Willie Taplin Barrow, fondly known as the "little warrior" who is chair of the board of the Rainbow Push Coalition. She has been a major player in both the Civil Rights movement and national and world politics, has led labor movements, and has been the catalyst for change in major corporations across this country.

The images and pictures that come to mind when we think "leader" speak volumes about our unspoken—yet prevailing—ideals of leadership. If we want to expand our concept of leadership, we need to expand our images of who and what a leader is.

The Language and Metaphors of Leadership

How we talk about leadership reinforces our understanding of leadership. We have specialized language to describe the actions of a leader, words such as "directs," "coaches," "guides," or "pilots." We use metaphors to convey the image of leader, such as "commander," "captain," "shepherd," "helmsman," "father," or "commander." Leaders are said to "take charge," to "take the bull by the horns," or to "rally the troops." For many people, to lead means "to direct," "to authorize," "to give orders," "to command," "to maneuver," "to manipulate." The very terms "leader, leading, and leadership" are traditionally packed with male images and ideas, with the leaders always seeming to be doing something *to* others, rarely doing things *with* others.

It is time to open the bottles or "skins" of leadership and add female concepts. This does not mean discarding male language, but rather elevating female language to the same level, to empower a broader understanding of the leadership phenomenon. As transformational leadership challenges the traditional terminology that has excluded women—as well as reinforced one-way, directive leadership styles—the wineskins are bursting. It is time for new containers that can stretch to carry the full flavor of leadership.

Reflection and Discussion Questions

1. Who or what comes to your mind when you think of "leader"?

2. As a young girl, who were the influential women in your church or community? What did you admire about them? What did you think of them at that time? How do you think of them now? How did your family, church, or community recognize influential women?

3. Have you ever tried to be "one of the boys" in order to be recognized or heard? What was that experience like for you?

4. Are there times when you have been put down for acting "just like a woman"? What was your reaction?

5. Have you been in a position of influence without a formal title of "leader"? What words would you use to describe your own leadership?

6. In what ways do you fit, or not fit, traditional notions of leadership?

The Leader as Midwife

Chapter 2

Puah and Shiphrah—
The Midwives Who Led
a Resistance*

The black communities of the Sea Islands of South Carolina have traditions that can be traced back to the days of slavery and linked to West African customs. In researching the evolution of their leadership practices, I asked some people of these small islands to describe the roles historically considered to be positions of leadership in their community. Over and over their responses pointed to the preacher and the politician. The preacher, who has served as a predominant leader in black communities from days of slavery, and the politician, from the days following the Emancipation and after the Civil Rights Era, have traditionally been men. When asked whether women held any leadership positions in the community, one person tentatively offered, "Well, maybe the midwives." She quickly qualified her response: "They weren't really leaders, though. But they were important to the community."

Even though they did not categorize midwives as leaders, I was intrigued by their description of the midwife's role in the community. She clearly had a life-changing and life-preserving influence. This simple portrayal of transformative leadership was the beginning of

* *The account of Puah and Shiphrah's leadership can be found in Exodus 1.*

my quest to understand the role of the midwife as a model for women's leadership. Because of the intricate network of relationships that midwives had with the women of a community, they were—and often still are—in a position to influence women. Not only was a midwife instrumental in the birthing process, but she also led a family through the natural and spiritual process that moved toward a healthy and safe delivery.

Prior to contemporary medical practices, helping women through the birthing process was considered to be the domain of women.[1] The tradition of midwifery is a long and enduring one, and the principles and practices of a midwife's trade have varied little for centuries. Midwives were described in biblical times (e.g., Genesis 35:17; Exodus 1:15-21) and were common in ancient Greece. Even in eighteenth and nineteenth century America, midwifery was a vital career for women, and until the early twentieth century, midwives attended nearly all births.[2]

In her book *Mama Day*, Gloria Naylor gives us a peak into the prominence of midwives in traditional communities and the link they provided among the people. Miranda, better known as Mama Day, was the island midwife who delivered babies on Willow Springs for three generations. After countless deliveries, Mama Day had become intimately aware of family matters and had learned to take appropriate and decisive action in all types of deliveries. Using natural medicines and spiritual wisdom, she cared for the members of the community and was considered a healer of the community.[3]

The aim of the midwife was to facilitate life. She was trained to serve as a catalyst for the mother's body chemistry and a guide to help the laboring woman use her energy wisely. Through experience and inherited wisdom,

a midwife learned what to do to accommodate the com-
plexities of birth and how to use the power of touch and
communication to guide the mother through the process.
She recognized the imminent signs of life and used both
her hands and her voice to help the mother remain calm
and to participate with the forces imploding upon her. She
reassured the mother that the baby would come forth in
due time. Believing fear to be the most contagious disease
to infect a laboring woman, the midwife communicated
peace and relaxation, stressing there was no need to be
afraid or to be in a hurry. She expected the birth to go right.
The midwife's focus was on the whole woman, not just the
birth canal.

Through the years, women and families came to
trust the midwife of the community, and their relationship
with the midwife did not end once a child was born. Midwives often delivered multiple babies for the same family
and provided ongoing healthcare for families in traditional
communities. Midwives felt called into their profession,
and many considered it both a spiritual and physical voca-
tion.[4]

The Early Practitioners of Midwifery

In the Old Testament Book of Exodus, we are introduced to some very early practitioners of the ancient art
of midwifery: Puah and Shiphrah. Their very names spoke
of their craft. Both names are thought to be of Egyptian origin: *Puah*, meaning "childbearing or joy of parents," and
Shiphrah, meaning "prolific" or "to procreate." These two
women are said to have been overseers of more than five
hundred midwives who worked throughout ancient
Egypt.[5] Most likely Puah and Shiphrah had established a

powerful reputation as midwives and had been elevated to official governmental positions.

At the time of their biblical story, tensions had arisen between two groups: the people of the dominant Egyptian culture *vs.* the people who had descended from Joseph. Joseph hailed from an ethnic or family group who had Semitic roots and whose distinguishing identity was their worship of Yahweh. Some four hundred years before, because of sibling rivalry and jealousy, Joseph had been sold as a slave and spent years in exile from his family, working as a house boy in the home of an Egyptian official. As a result of false accusations, he was later imprisoned for a number of years, but miraculously ended up being appointed Minister of Operations by Pharaoh, the King of Egypt. Overnight Joseph rose in prominence and influence as second in command to the Pharaoh.

Because of Joseph's foresighted efforts to save Egypt from massive famine, Pharaoh gave permission for Joseph's entire extended family to join him in Egypt. Although welcomed at first, no doubt benefiting from the rank and stature of their now-favored relative, the situation changed over the years. By the time of Puah and Shiphrah, the descendants of Joseph had grown into a sizable minority group and had come to be seen as a threat by the current Pharaoh. With the changing of the guard came a changing of policies and rules. Choosing to disregard the long-standing national policies that permitted the Israelites to exist in peace in Egypt, the current Pharaoic administration created new domestic policies that, in essence, enslaved the children of Israel, targeting them as the labor source for extensive civic construction projects. Fearing this burgeoning minority might grow large enough to join forces with another national power in revolt, the Egyptian leadership decided to take drastic steps to reduce the birth rate: Pharaoh commanded the midwives to determine the sex of the baby when they saw the Hebrew mothers give birth on the birth stools (Exodus 1:16) and to kill all the baby boys.

It appears that Pharaoh wanted the midwives to collude in his plan by attributing these infant deaths to complications at birth. The plan may have called for them not to cut the umbilical cord in time, or not to clear the throat, or in some way to smother the baby boy. The plan certainly called for the midwives to withhold care from any baby boy before the mother could realize what was going on or intervene or call for help. The aim of this plan—population control—was the same combination of extreme ethnocentrism and protection of power that is at the core of ethnic cleansing campaigns down through the ages, even in our contemporary world.

Perhaps these extreme orders were fed by xenophobia, a fear and hatred of difference. Perhaps the administrations' fears were supported by the fact that Egypt was involved in extensive military campaigns that left a large portion of its military power stationed outside of the country. Whatever the motivating fears, the new policies issued by the administration crept into the domain and work of Puah and Shiphrah. It was their responsibility to systematically limit the births of the growing ethnic minority.

Although the authority to carry out these orders rested in the hands of these two women, they would have had to execute this genocidal campaign through the intricate network of midwives, since they most likely did not personally attend all births. How could Puah and Shiphrah, who had devoted their lives and professions to bringing forth life, now participate in extinguishing it? They were put in an untenable situation: to obey an order that conflicted with their professional and moral values, or to obey their conscience and risk losing their jobs—perhaps even their lives. And even if they refused to execute this policy, no doubt Pharaoh would have elevated some other accomplices to carry out his plan of destruction. Clearly Puah and Shiphrah faced a difficult leadership challenge.

Their courageous decision is recorded in Exodus 1:17: *"The midwives, however, feared God and did not do what the King of Egypt had told them to do; they let the boys live."*

The Principles of Midwifery

The key principles and practices of midwifery provide a lens for understanding the actions Puah and Shiphrah took, both as midwives and as leaders of other midwives. As midwives, they had come to know and respect the birth process, to honor the unseen forces of life neither they nor the delivering mother could control. As midwives, they yielded to those life forces and taught the birthing mother to do likewise. As they entered into one of the most intimate aspects of a woman's being, they developed a strong relationship with the birthing mother. When midwives were invited into the birthing chamber, the most private corner of a woman's home, the mother was laid bare, exposed and vulnerable. Between the intense moments of contractions and labor pains, no doubt the midwife and mother talked of very personal things, perhaps sharing stories of past births, personal challenges, and triumphs. Midwife and mother stole glimpses into each other's lives in a most intimate manner.

I can't help but believe that during those laboring times many Hebrew women talked of and even cried out to their God Yahweh. Perhaps it was in that inner sanctum of the birthing chamber that midwives acquired a deep respect for the God of the Hebrews, for Scripture reminds us that "the midwives feared God" (Exodus 1:17). The Hebrew word *yare*, translated as "fear" in this passage, carries a double connotation: *Yare* means to fear or be afraid of something, as well as to stand in awe or revere someone or something that holds great power.[6] Perhaps these midwives stood in awe of God because they had come to associate the Hebrew God with the unseen forces of life to which they had grown accustomed to yielding. Certainly their respect for God deepened their value for life and the spiritual forces behind it and must have influenced their decision not to participate in Pharaoh's plan of genocide. Yet the question remains: How did these midwives single-handedly stop the campaign to kill male children?

The Plan of Resistance

The culmination of the midwifing process focuses on the final phase of the pregnancy, during those last few days, hours, and minutes of labor. When the cramping, contractions, and breaking of the water sac signal that the baby is coming, a mother has to get into position to give birth and concentrate all her energies on pushing the baby through the birth canal.

Typically, a midwife would be called in by the birthing mother or by members of her family as the woman went into labor. As the forces of life brought forth the baby, the midwife would wait with the mother, calming her fears and facilitating her through the process. While no one can predict how long a woman will be in labor, I am sure these midwives knew how to time their arrival at the birthing chamber to optimize their role in the birthing process.

Midwives often used "birth stools" to help make that work a little easier and efficient. These stools—which may have been an Egyptian invention[7]—were stone chairs that enabled a laboring woman to remain upright during the delivery so she could optimize the forces of gravity. Though the upward position increased the risk of tearing during birth, the position was believed to quicken the final phase of delivery by taking advantage of the downward pull of gravity.

The first clue we get to Puah's and Shiphrah's insubordination lies in the Egyptian Pharaoh's instructions. Pharaoh commanded, "When you help the Hebrew women in childbirth and observe them on the delivery stool, if it is a boy kill him; but if it is a girl, let her live" (Exodus 1:16). Ironically, the king's own command may have set up the conditions for the midwives' strategic waiting to be effective.

These midwives knew that the babies would come forth with or without the presence of a midwife. Their absence could not hinder the birth, yet because of the genocidal order, their presence could potentially do more harm than good. So they strategically arrived too late to carry out the king's edict. By the time a birthing mother was "on the birthing stool," the mother would have been in full-blown labor and the baby near birth. Under those conditions, it would have been difficult to dispose of the baby boy without the mother's knowledge.

I can't help but believe that Puah and Shiphrah and their band of midwives now waited *for* the birthing mother instead of waiting *with* the birthing mothers. I can't help but believe that these wise women timed their arrivals in such a way that they were present to care for mother and baby well after the baby's sex had been declared, and too late to clandestinely dispose of the baby without mother or other family members intervening.

I envision a network of midwives practicing the art of resistance, of strategic waiting. I imagine them learning to trust a process which they had for years taught birthing mothers to trust. I see a quiet band of resistors who learned valuable lessons of faith while fulfilling their duties as midwives. We may never know exactly how Puah and Shiphrah and the hundreds of midwives who worked for them were able to remove themselves from the birthing process until well after the newborn baby boys were safe in their mother's arms. However, we do know when word reached Pharaoh that the boys were not being killed, he summoned Puah and Shiphrah and demanded an answer.

The midwives' response was to give the king insight into the differences in birthing conditions between Hebrew and Egyptian women. "Hebrew women are not like the Egyptian women; for they are vigorous and give birth before the midwives arrive" (Exodus 1:19). This gives us a glimpse of Puah and Shiphrah's courage. Their response subtly suggested that this was information Pharaoh *should* have known. Apparently their strategy worked, for Pharaoh dropped the campaign, at least temporarily. The Hebrew women continued giving birth, and their people continued to become even more numerous (Genesis 1:20).

We may never know how many young boys were saved as a result of Puah and Shiphrah's passive resistance, but the Scripture text reminds us that Puah and Shiphrah and their band of midwives were blessed by God for their action—or, in this case, their strategic *inaction*. Because these midwives respected God, God honored them by giving them families of their own.

Puah and Shiphrah are a testament to the power and influence of transformative leaders. They serve as models not only of women well trained in their profession who provide a model for other professional women, but also as women of faith. They took the risk to do a righteous thing. They helped turn a bleak situation into a blessing for the Hebrew mothers, as well as for themselves. Their acts of resistance set the tone for the broader works of resistance that would occur later when Pharaoh gave a new edict to *all* the people, not just the midwives, to kill Hebrew baby boys. Their leadership created the conditions that would allow the future leader of Israel, Moses, to survive as a Hebrew boy and grow to become the deliverer of his people from their bondage under Pharaoh.

Reflection and Discussion Questions

1. As you reflect on the story of Puah and Shiphrah, consider their leadership qualities. What women do you know who have these qualities? Which of these qualities are characteristic of you?

2. If you have given birth, what aspects of other people's care and support were most helpful to you? If you have been close to someone giving birth, what have you done to be supportive and encouraging? What do you think was most helpful?

3. Think of a time when you found yourself in a situation that conflicted with your values. What choices did you face? What did you choose to do? What was the outcome? Now that you have read Puah and Shiphrah's story, what might you do next time you are faced with such a challenging situation?

4. Have you ever been in a situation where "strategic waiting" was the best strategy? Reflect on your action, or *inaction* as is the case. How did it influence the eventual outcome?

Chapter 3

The Leader as Midwife

I love listening to Bishop Carlton Pearson's stories about the "old folks." The old folks were the men and women of his cultural tradition who instilled within him fervency for God and helped him to understand and appreciate his godly heritage. These folks saw God-given talents in young people and encouraged their growth, "midwifing" his generation.

Bishop Pearson reminisces about Old Mother Sherman, a district missionary and "a powerful, preaching woman" who encouraged and admonished him from the time he was a young boy. Starting when he was about age four or five, Mother Sherman would approach him and ask, "Son, you yet holdin' on?"

Young Carlton would reply, "Yes ma'am, I'm yet holdin' on."

Mother Sherman's admonishment back to him would be, "Well, then keep on keepin' on." And she would give him a nickel.

As young Carlton grew, Mother Sherman regularly encouraged him with "Keep on keepin' on" and progressed from giving him a nickel, to giving him a dime, then a quarter and so forth. By the time Carlton was about to go off to college, he recalls that Mother Sherman was still encouraging him with "You keep on keepin' on" and he was up to a dollar. Clearly the words "keep on keepin' on" were more valuable than the coins and remained with him much longer.[1]

I remember the "old folks" in my life, too: the people who helped facilitate the birth of a dream, the growth of a spiritually mature person. These old leaders of the church served as midwives to a host of boys and girls, men and women whose dreams of a brighter day otherwise may have been aborted. They encouraged us with their stern admonishments. They encouraged us with their songs of hope. They taught us how to fast and pray. They taught us about the things of God and helped to build up our faith.

Such people of encouragement sometimes surface in unexpected places. I remember Nancy, the director of corporate staff human resources at the company where I took my first full-time professional job. I was not long out of graduate school when I started working as an internal organizational development consultant. My manager had been a little hesitant to hire me because, in his opinion, I was not "seasoned" enough to be a corporate consultant. He eventually agreed to bring me on as an associate, with the promise of a performance review and, contingent upon performance, promotion into a full-fledged consultant role after nine months.

The corporate culture of that company was "old school" manufacturing; most of the managers had risen up through the ranks from the local or regional mills and plants. The managers were professional, political—and mostly male. Each plant, regional office, or mill had its own culture, and people in each location were extremely loyal to the local unit. Corporate staffers were often seen as the "enemy" by local employees and managers. I found the work rewarding but learning to navigate the complex culture was challenging.

Although I was assigned to work with Nancy only a few times, I had to pass her corner office on my way to the ladies' room or the copy room. She would call me in occasionally to "see how things were going." Nancy was always encouraging and frequently provided me with positive feedback. She would share with me positive comments she had heard about my work out in the field and would give me background information on people I was scheduled to meet. On the few occasions that we were all in town, Nancy, two other women, and I would go to lunch together.

After my first nine months on the job, I asked for the promised performance review. I believed I was performing well and did not warrant the junior status in the department any longer. My boss readily admitted he had underestimated me and promoted me to consultant.

Given the intricate political structure of that company, I could have died prematurely in a non-nurturing and unconfirming environment. Instead, I blossomed and performed well. Looking back on that experience, I now realize that Nancy served as midwife to me. She helped facilitate the birth of the corporate consultant that I became. Though we did not spend huge amounts of time working together, she saw the potential in me and encouraged me to achieve my goals. She took time to inquire about my work and progress, and she listened intently to me. She helped me to consider longer-range career options and frequently shared her own story about her corporate career path.

There were times we just talked about shopping and our wardrobes (she was an avid shopper). When we traveled to several conferences together, she gave me simple travel tips that made my corporate travel easier—such as never wear the same pair of shoes two days in a row in humid cities or heavy walking situations. That one small piece of advice alone saved my feet for many years to come!

It was also Nancy who opened the door for my first community consulting experience. She was on the board of directors for the local YWCA and invited me to join her in conducting team-building activities for the board and staff. This experience helped lay the foundation for my belief that providing service to the community is part and parcel of being a well-rounded consultant. Her influence carried over in later years as I became involved in two other community non-profit agencies and participated in a regional leadership development program sponsored by the Urban League.

So what do the "old folks" in Bishop Pearson's life, Mother Sherman, and Nancy have in common? As midwives, they shared several key qualities: they recognized pregnant possibilities; they helped create conditions for birthing through their words of encouragement; they provided care and nurture through relationship; and they understood the delicate process and timing of birthing.

Recognizing Pregnant Possibilities

Midwives as leaders can be found in every facet of life. Teachers, for example, can be midwives guiding students to birth dreams and develop into life-long learners capable of succeeding in a variety of environments. Teachers have a unique opportunity to nurture the first signs of intellectual interest in a particular subject and help students become aware of their potential. Too many of our young people have been written off by authority figures and make choices that limit their effectiveness. They may have become labeled as troublemakers, belligerent, obstinate, while their potential remains untapped. Their pregnant possibilities may die without the touch of a gifted midwife, and teachers serve in this important role.

The entrepreneur can be a midwife as well, guiding the growth of a start-up company into a successful business. The entrepreneur sees the possibilities of her product or service and works relentlessly to nourish the enterprise, fund it, and search out new customer bases. Developing the business plan, finding appropriate funding sources, test-marketing her ideas, recruiting partners and employees who also see the possibilities are midwifery functions necessary for the survival of the embryonic business.

Business and corporate leaders can be midwives, too, birthing both business enterprises and other business leaders. Many top leaders today acknowledge the role that one of their managers played in their own development and growth as a leader. Since the success of the business or organization depends on being able to fill openings with good talent and being able to match leadership strength with the needs of the organization, midwife managers learn to spot potential talent and nurture the achievements of promising leaders.

Ministry leaders, too, can be midwives, helping to birth other leaders. When a youth pastor ministers to young people, for example, teaching biblical principles and transmitting spiritual values, that pastor is not only helping the young person come to understand her own identity, purpose, and gifts but is also recognizing and encouraging that person's leadership potential.

I'll never forget my experience with a young man named Bryan. He had been attending meetings of a young people's organization of which I was a youth leader. I had heard him sing at a few local services (you should have heard him sing our "theme song" in his smooth, beautiful voice!), and I asked if he would consider being part of the team that led worship at the beginning of each service. He enthusiastically committed himself to the team and eventually joined the leadership training. After my term in office was over, Bryan continued working with the organization and eventually was asked to join a national Christian recording group. Oftentimes when the group comes to Chicago, he invites me to attend their concerts. When I met him back stage once, Bryan introduced me to his fellow band members as "the woman who gave me my first start." I had no idea about the impact my early youth ministry days had had on Bryan. His mother told me later she had known that Bryan had lots of potential but that he had needed the extra "push" I had given him. Being able to recognize undeveloped ability is an important midwifery quality. The midwife leader sees the possibilities that others do not seem to notice, or that a person cannot see for herself.

Creating Conditions for Birth through Words of Encouragement

At a small eastern liberal arts college there is a teacher named Gina who is a midwife to students underutilizing their potential. Over and over she sees young people making choices that undermine their success, remaining in relationships that are harmful or hanging out with friends instead of studying. But instead of seeing failures, she sees people who have not received the encouragement they need to meet their full potential.

Gina's story of a bright young woman named Ivory illustrate what a midwife leader does. Ivory was working her way through college and was in a relationship with a young man who demanded much of her time. Her boyfriend had been the subject of numerous disciplinary actions, and a number of the school administrators had noted the effect of his behavior on Ivory. Gina had seen Ivory around campus quite a bit but did not have the opportunity to interact with her until Gina was assigned as Ivory's new academic advisor. Gina recalls, "When I received her dismal midterm grade report, I called Ivory in to see me. I prayed for just the right words to say."

After they discussed her academic progress, Gina gently shared an observation that caught Ivory off guard: "Ivory, you are a bright person. You have lots of potential."

Ivory shook her head slightly, looked down, shrugged her head, and muttered, "I guess I do all right in the things I like."

Gina smiled back at her and remarked, "I've seen your ACT scores. I know you have the ability. If you do well only in the things you like, perhaps it's an issue of discipline, not of capability. You can do this work. You have it in you."

Ivory was stone silent but continued to look at Gina. It appeared that few people had ever told her that she was capable.

Gina continued, "Ivory, I am not trying to preach to you, but I am concerned and want you to know that I know you can do better. But you have to figure out what *Ivory* wants and what is good for *Ivory*. You see to everyone else and you fail to develop healthy boundaries. In the long run those choices are hurting you. You have a lot going for you and God has blessed you."

Ivory looked at Gina and quietly said, "Thank you for taking the time to care."

Gina had done more than recognize the potential in this young woman. At a time critical to Ivory's future, Gina stepped in to help create supportive conditions in which Ivory could examine her choices from a different perspective. This midwife leader's words of encouragement helped to birth an Ivory who was less of a people-pleaser and more of a young woman who could cherish her God-given gifts.

Providing Care and Nurture through Relationship

Arly was another one of Gina's students. A beautiful young woman with tremendous potential for leading others, Arly often displayed a beautiful, bright smile. Yet a closer look revealed a slight strain behind that smile and the confusion in her eyes.

In particular, Gina noticed that when she complimented Arly, Arly would seem uncomfortable, shyly looking down and averting eye contact. One day Gina asked her, "What do you think about yourself, and what do you hear inside your head when you are complimented?"

Arly started off quietly and as she continued with her response, tears welled up in her eyes. "I hear what my Mom used to always call me. She said I was no good. I was a b----. She told my sisters and me that all the time. 'You girls ain't s---. Just a bunch of whores.'" Arly described how she had been sexually abused as a child by one of her mother's boyfriends and how often she had felt neglected, even abandoned, by her drug-addicted mother. She told Gina she had been "saved" as a teen and that God had changed her life, but she was still plagued by self-doubt and anger.

Though her life was playing out differently from what her mother had predicted, Arly was not able to fully accept or believe that she was a good person worthy of good things happening to her. She had not been able to replace the damning messages stored in the tape recorder of her mind and was still haunted by the messages of past condemnation.

Gina recalls, "I began praying for Arly to be free from the binding memories and thoughts that plagued her. I began teaching her how to expose the lie of those past messages and replace them with the truth. I continually encouraged her to see herself as God saw her and kept affirming what I saw in her. This gifted young woman began to blossom. And the more other people saw of her potential, the more she blossomed."

With her constancy and support, Gina modeled a new type of relationship for Arly: a relationship of consistency and affirmation. With Gina's encouragement, Arly got additional help from the campus counseling center, and Gina remained available to Arly for talks, prayer, and sharing. As Arly grew and developed a strong network of friends, she came to rely on Gina less and discover her own gifts more. Eventually, Arly assumed a community ministry leadership position and grew into a spiritually mature young woman. The care and nurture of Gina's midwifing had had helped birth a new leader.

Understanding the Timing and Process of Birthing

One of the most crucial skills of the midwife leader is the ability to understand both the birth process and its timing. Just as the midwife comes to understand

and participate with the forces of life, so the midwife leader comes to understand that God, the Force of all life, the Giver of all potential and gifts, is working in her own life and in the lives of the people around her. As the midwife learns to trust the process, knowing that neither she nor the birthing mother can control the timing of birth, so the leader who midwives learns that she cannot control the growth and development of the people whom she serves as midwife. The midwife leader participates in a grand and glorious scheme larger than she is.

The midwife leader understands that birthing strong healthy women and men of faith is a process that takes time. Too often we expect the people we mentor or coach to develop in the same time frame in which we developed or to conform to a culturally established norm. The spiritual midwife recognizes that God places us in the lives of people to help them connect with their purpose and cultivate their gifts in their own way and time.

The midwife leader also understands that each birth is different, that each person is different, that each person's development and growth is in the hands of the Force of all life. By letting go of attempts to control a process that is ultimately beyond her dominion, the midwife leader is freed up to facilitate, pray, and nurture the unique growth of each individual.

Pushing through the Pain

I have been blessed to have a number of midwives assist me at various stages of my development. From my mother and aunts, to older women at my church during my college days, many women have helped to birth the leader I have become. One particular midwife in my life is a woman who provided care for me during the hustle and bustle of my young professional life when I failed to adequately care for myself. Though I had been experiencing painful menstrual periods for some time, I had ignored the pain—I was a "strong black woman" who could "handle" the pain.

Eventually, I was diagnosed with fibroid tumors that had to be removed surgically. (Today, women suffering from fibroid tumors have far more options—including laser surgery and procedures to shrink the tumors.) Back then, the doctors and I wondered if perhaps the fibroid tumors had been caught sooner, the surgery would not have been necessary. Unfortunately, once the doctors attempted to remove the tumors, they found six tumors the size of grapefruits in my uterus. My doctors and those close to me were particularly sensitive to the fact that I was a young, unmarried woman in prime childbearing age. They tried everything possible but could not salvage my situation. They had to remove my entire uterus and, at twenty-eight-years old, any possibility of birthing children was taken away with that damaged organ.

I am grateful to the many people who prayed for me and offered words of encouragement during that time. One woman, Roseann Pratt, stands out to me now as a midwife who helped me push through the pain and recover from this trauma. In addition to being the wife of a prominent pastor, Evangelist Pratt was also a renowned preacher and community leader.

At the time of the diagnosis, I had been living by myself as an independent professional woman. My mother had joined me for the surgery, but due to a series of surgeries of her own, she had to return home within a few days. When my mother left, Sister Pratt, as we affectionately called her, insisted there was no way I was going to be able to care for myself during the two-month recuperative period after surgery, and brought me to her home to recuperate.

Although the physical pain was excruciating, the emotional pain was equally intense. Even as late as the late 1980s, so much of a woman's identity was attached to her ability to bear children. It seemed that a woman could *choose* not to bear children, but a woman who *could* not bear children was seen as inadequate—or so I believed.

So for many a night Sister Pratt and I talked. She shared her own stories of testing and trials and triumph. I prayed and I cried out to God. Once I was walking again and was able to get out of the house a little bit, my first trip to the grocery store left me sobbing in the aisle of the Hallmark card section. It was the Mother's Day season, and the entire aisle of cards was a reminder to me of what I had just lost. I grieved that loss right there in the store as all the pent-up emotions seemed to gush out.

Deep down I had wanted to have children, and I was struggling with my new reality. I began to repeat Sister Pratt's words from a sermon as my mantra: "My life is in God's hands." Eventually the intense emotions subsided, and I began to make sense out of what was happening to me and to trust God with this situation.

I remember one evening in particular when Sister Pratt quietly brought an extremely touching and timely card to my room. On the front cover was an illustration of a group of men raising the thatched roof of a little hut so they could lower a man down inside. The caption read, "Some friends who care about you are raising the roof on your behalf." While the card referred to Zaccheus' friends who cared about him enough to carry him to Jesus, I knew that Sister Pratt and others were "raising the roof" for me, crying out to heaven on my behalf.

I realize now that Sister Pratt had recognized God's hand on my life and knew intuitively that this painful situation had the potential to distract me from my calling. She recognized me as a leader-in-the-making. Although I was already serving in leadership positions, she knew something more was waiting to be birthed in and through me.

Too often leaders have no one to help them through painful experiences. Embryonic leaders who face crisis or are hurting, and who do not receive proper spiritual care are at risk of being aborted. As a midwife, Sister Pratt helped to create conditions for a new me—a new perspective and a new level of faith—to be birthed from my pain. Always ready with words of advice and encouragement, Sister Pratt continues to share with me her wisdom and provides timely guidance for ministry even today.

My relationship with this spiritual midwife helped turn something painful into something powerful. This crisis brought me closer to God and helped me to connect with the transformative purposes of my own life. Although birthing children in traditional ways was not to be a part of my destiny path, this process helped to birth a person who would come to birth spiritual children. As college professor, preacher, auntie, godmother, and friend I have had the joy of helping others birth their potential, of seeing girls and boys grow, women and men develop.

As women, many of us have faced some physical or emotional crisis related to our gender. We live in a world that has not always cherished girls or womanhood, so too many of us have suffered at the hands of people who have told us that we could not reach our dreams. Too many of us have been told about our limitations rather than our possibilities. Too many of us have been abused by harsh words or crushed by physical blows. Too many women have been raped by overpowering men or women. Too many women have been treated unjustly in inequitable systems where work rules, the legal system, and cultural norms have kept us on the margins of power.

Perhaps you have experienced some personal trauma that has left you wounded. Perhaps you have felt that your dreams died because of a trauma in your life. These experiences, no matter how painful, do not negate the reality of your calling; rather they can be a part of shaping you, helping you become who you were called to become. Maybe you need someone to help midwife you through your pain. Maybe your experience with pain has put you in a position to midwife another woman through her pain.

Called to Midwife

The midwife leader patiently waits for the birthing of greatness, encouraging and helping to build the faith of the people she assists. The midwife leader helps calm the fears of the people she assists and motivates them to do and be more than they could do and be on their own. The midwife leader understands the importance of the lives she touches and the significance of her touch on the lives of other people.

Opportunities to midwife present themselves every day.

Some of you are in contact with girls and boys, women and men, who never had a strong sense of self instilled within them. Perhaps you can see the potential in a young woman, and you have been placed in her life to facilitate the birthing of that potential.

Some of you know people who have the seeds of dreams and ideas that need to be nurtured and developed into reality.

Some of you have been called to lead the work in bringing about change for a more just organization or society.

Some of you are being called to be a woman of influence, a transformative leader, to midwife some new project in your community.

Some of you serve in formal positions of leadership and have people on your team, on your staff, or in your department that have vast potential waiting to be birthed.

Some of you may need a midwife leader to help you give birth to the dream that is in you. Some of you are being transformed so that you may help to transform others.

Pray about and consider where you are being called to midwife.

Reflection and Discussion Questions

1. Who have you known who had the skills of a midwife? What did they do to help birth other people or dreams?

2. Has anyone ever midwifed you, physically, emotionally, or spiritually? How have they made a difference in your life?

3. In what ways do you currently midwife others, helping them give birth to their ideas and dreams?

4. Who do you see around you that has untapped potential? Can you think of someone in whose life God has placed you to help midwife? What are the signs of "pregnant" possibilities you see in this person? In what ways can you provide nurture and care to this person?

The Leader as Choreographer

Chapter 4

Miriam—The Dancing Leader[*]

Many people know about the liberating leadership of Moses—the man God called to challenge the Egyptian Pharaoh and set in motion the exodus of the Hebrew nation from slavery. So powerful was his leadership that thousands of years later he is held in reverence by both Jews and Christians. So powerful was his legacy that African slaves in nineteenth century America trusted the God of Moses to likewise free them from their bondage.[1]

Fewer people know of another great leader and member of Moses' leadership team—his sister, Miriam (I Chronicles 6:3). Israel's deliverance from slavery is attributed to the leadership of Moses, Aaron, *and* Miriam. God reminded the people of Israel of this through the prophet Micah: "I brought you up out of Egypt and redeemed you from the land of slavery. I sent Moses to lead you, also Aaron and Miriam" (Micah 6:4). While the roles played by Moses and Aaron are well known, few of us realize the important role Miriam played in the redemptive history of the nation of Israel.

Daughter of Destiny

Miriam was Moses' older sister and is thought to have been about seven years old when he was born. Moses' birth occurred during the perilous times of Pharaoh's cam-

---

The account of Miriam's leadership can be found in Exodus 2 and 15, and Numbers 12.

paign to kill all Hebrew baby boys. Although the midwives Puah and Shiphrah had staved off the first threat, the Pharaoh had proceeded to command *all* the citizens of Egypt to drown Hebrew baby boys in the Nile River. Any male child born to a Hebrew woman was born to a death warrant. No doubt Hebrew mothers tried every means possible to protect and hide their baby boys.

Jochebed, a woman married to a priest named Amram, was such a mother. She had given birth to her third child during the era of Pharaoh's campaign of infanticide and had managed to keep her pregnancy and birth secret in defiance of Pharaoh's edict. However, as the baby boy grew, it was harder to keep him hidden from the vigilant Egyptian eyes searching for Hebrew baby boys.

When Moses was about three months old, Jochebed took an action of faith that sealed the fate of her baby boy (Hebrews 11:23). Rather than see her infant son torn from her arms by the hated henchmen of Pharaoh's command, Jochebed prepared a papyrus basket, applying pitch and tar to waterproof it. She wrapped her precious son in blankets, placed him into the basket, and nestled the bundle among the reeds along the bank of the Nile River. As she departed, leaving the baby's older sister, Miriam, hiding in the shadows to watch what happened, I am sure she prayed and put the fate of her baby in Yahweh's hands.

As the baby boy lay floating among the reeds, Pharaoh's daughter, who had come down to the Nile to bathe, caught a glimpse of the basket and sent her servant girl to retrieve it. When the princess opened the basket and saw the baby, who by this time was crying, she correctly surmised that the boy was a Hebrew child. Before any action or decisions could be made, out from the shadows came young Miriam, mindful of her baby brother's needs and ready to influence the princess on her brother's behalf. What we see next in Miriam's story is an artful choreographing of a strategic "dance" that brought Jochebed and Pharaoh's daughter together and ultimately determined Moses' destiny.

I can see the young Miriam tentatively, respectfully approaching the princess. Surely the princess must have realized that this young Hebrew girl knew the little boy and knew who his mother was. And Miriam must have realized that the crying baby had already touched the heart of the princess; somehow she knew that the princess was not going to drown her baby brother. In fact, the princess was giving indications she would keep the baby for herself. If that were the case, the boy would need to be properly nursed, so Miriam boldly queried the princess, perhaps even planting an idea in the princess's mind: "Shall I go and get one of the Hebrew women to nurse the baby for you?" With the princess' acquiescence, young Miriam scurried off to find her mother.

As Miriam was leading Jochebed back to the riverbank, I can almost hear her proclaiming, "Mother, it is a miracle. Pharaoh's daughter will not destroy the baby. She has had mercy on him and is seeking a nurse maid for him. My brother is safe!"

When Jochebed approached, the princess gave her a simple order: "Go and nurse this baby for me, and I will pay you." The princess must have realized that, by issuing such a command, she was defying her own father's edict. "Surely," she might have mused to herself, "my father's edict does not apply to me. I am his princess and he will bend his rule for me—that is, if he ever finds out this baby's origin." By commanding Jochebed to nurse the baby for pay, the princess entered into a contractual relationship of sorts that not only rendered the baby's death warrant null and void but also ensured that Jochebed could safely nurse the baby in the comfort of her home until he was old enough to be officially adopted by the princess and live in the palace. In honor of the means and place from which she found her newly adopted son, the princess named the baby Moses, which means "drawn out of the water" (Exodus 2:10).

Young Miriam's role in Moses' rescue poses an interesting thought: How many of us, like Miriam, gave indication of our leadership potential very early in life? For some, it might have surfaced in our oratorical skills, as we recited poetry and other speeches before our church and civic clubs. On the school grounds at recess, others of us initiated the games, serving as ring leader whom other girls and boys followed. Unfortunately, too many people miss the signs of leadership in young girls and fail to develop or midwife that talent. Perhaps Miriam's story will open your eyes to the young Miriams in your life.

This young seven-year-old was in no position to save her brother directly nor did she have any overt power to tell the princess or Jochebed what to do. Instead, Miriam watched, remaining vigilant for an opportunity to intervene. She then helped connect the princess with Jochebed, planting ideas within both their hearts for the care of Moses. Perhaps if Miriam had not remained near her brother, the princess would have found the abandoned baby boy and, out of compassion, saved him anyway. She even might have found an Egyptian nursemaid to care for the baby. Yet Miriam's timing and boldness in offering a suggestion influenced the destiny of Moses, enabling him to remain with his own mother for a few more years. This early period of his life, before being transferred to the palace, no doubt helped shape his values and identity, both of which would become critical to him and to the nation of Israel in later years.

Precursors to Miriam's Leadership

The true leadership of Miriam remains invisible during the ensuing years leading up to the Exodus of the Israelites from the land of Egypt, and we need to track Moses' life to understand the significance of Miriam's re-entry into the story. After being raised in the royal palace, Moses began to realize his true ethnic identity and ventured out to see how the Hebrews lived. Once he grasped the horrible conditions under which his people existed, Moses, in a fit of rage, murdered an Egyptian who was beating a Hebrew.

The next day he saw a couple of Hebrew men fighting amongst themselves, and he challenged the aggressor, "Why are you hitting your fellow Hebrew?"

The Hebrew man retorted, "Who made you ruler and judge over us? Are you thinking of killing me as you killed the Egyptian?"

Though he wanted to identify with his Hebrew "brothers," Moses had not realized that he still retained the social privilege and trappings of an elite Egyptian. Worse yet, he had not realized that anyone had seen his murderous actions the day before. Realizing he could not establish solidarity with these two Hebrews and fearing he would be exposed, Moses fled Egypt. He ended up in a desert country called Midian and spent the next forty years in the household of Jethro, the priest of Midian. There he tended sheep, married Jethro's daughter Zipporah, and with Zipporah fathered two sons, Gershom and Eliezer (Exodus 18:3-4; Acts 7:29).

In the meantime, the current Pharaoh had died and the oppressive conditions of the Hebrews back in Egypt worsened. The children of Israel cried out to God and God heard their cries. God appeared to Moses in a burning bush and called Moses to return to Egypt to free his people from their oppression. After some coaxing and reassurance, Moses consented to go.

Moses, with his brother Aaron by his side, confronted the Pharaoh. What ensued was a series of spiritual signs underscoring the power of the God of Israel. After the final challenge of the death angel, in which every firstborn son of the Egyptians was killed, the Pharaoh and the people of Egypt urged Moses and the Hebrews to leave. In fact, so glad were they to have the Israelites gone, the Egyptians gave the Hebrews gifts of gold, silver, and clothing as they departed (Exodus 12:35).

Moses organized and led the massive numbers of Hebrews out of Egypt, following God's cloud by day and fiery pillar by night, around by the desert road toward Canaan—the land God had promised to their ancestor Abraham generations before. But all too soon, Pharaoh had second thoughts about letting the Hebrews, his slave labor, go. Although he had perceived them to be a threat, he began to see them as less of a threat within his own borders than outside his borders. So Pharaoh decided to send out his army to retrieve his runaway slaves who were, in his eyes, chattel or property.

As Pharaoh's army approached, the Hebrews were terrified. They never expected the Egyptians to come after them, and they felt ill-prepared to face their foe. The Egyptian army was advancing toward the Israelite camp from behind, and the Red Sea was blocking the passage ahead. They could see no way of escape. The people cried out to Moses, "Why didn't you just let us die in Egypt rather than bring us to our deaths out here in this desert?"

Moses, in faith proclaimed, "Do not be afraid. Stand firm and you will see the deliverance the Lord will bring you today. The Egyptians you see today you will never see again. The Lord will fight for you; you need only to be still" (Exodus 14:13-14).

Then the Lord commanded Moses, "Raise your staff and stretch out your hand over the sea to divide the water so that the Israelites can go through on dry ground." Throughout the night God led the Hebrews on dry ground through the parted sea and delivered them safe to the other side. Pharaoh's army was foiled in its attempts to re-capture this nation of God. When the Hebrews saw the great power of God displayed against the Egyptians, they reverenced God and put their trust, once again, in Yahweh and in Moses, the servant of God.

Throughout all of these episodes, we see no evidence of Miriam. Whatever leadership role she played in Egypt, her significance as a leader is not made clear until after the Hebrew people reached the other side of the Red Sea. It is then that Miriam's true leadership emerges.

The Leader of Dancers

After such a great escape and mighty display of power, the people of God were finally free. What did the people of God do when they realized that they were delivered from the land of bondage and from their captors? They praised their God and gave thanks for their liberation. And who led them in this song of triumph, exalting the Lord and commemorating the miraculous events that had just occurred? It was Miriam who took a tambourine in her hand and was inspired by God to lead the women in an exuberant and lively dance ritual, perhaps symbolizing the victory march of a conquering army. Their chorus rang out: "Sing to the Lord for he is highly exalted. The horse and its rider, he has hurled into the sea" (Exodus 15:21).

In the ancient world, where many battles took place, it was custom for the conquering commander to lead a victory processional of the military troops. The conquered army and the spoils of battle would normally trail behind the heroes. But in the case of the Hebrews, the conquered army was nowhere to be found and the spoils of war had been gained without any fighting. What Miriam did in her processional was to remind the people of the *spiritual* nature of their victory.

In all cultures, rituals are enactments that help bring meaning to significant events as well as mark transition points. For the Hebrews, Miriam's dance symbolized the end of their slavery and the beginning of a new life as liberated people. Miriam's processional marked the passage through the Sea—from Pharaoh's slaves to God's liberated people. Miriam's dance celebrated God's use of her brother as the instrument of freedom and God's seal on the fate of the Hebrews' antagonists. Never would they see those Egyptians again. Now that was definitely something to sing about!

Miriam reminded her people of the power and importance of celebration. Whatever other leadership roles she played in the redemption of the nation of Israel, this particular role is of utmost importance. She reminds us of the necessity of celebrating after all victories—no matter how large or small. Too often we take no breather between events in our rushed busy lives. We go from one crisis to another and never take time to commemorate the occasion, dance in celebration, or sing in thanks. Miriam's celebration reminds us of the scriptural mandate to "give thanks in all circumstances, for this is God's will for you in Christ Jesus" (I Thessalonians 5:18).

Miriam inspires us to dance, to raise our hands, and shout! Miriam's celebration also reminds us of the necessity of creating space between the ending of the old and the beginning of the new. We can never truly make a new start until we have adequately brought closure to an old phase. The celebration ritual marks the closure of the last campaign and prepares us for the next event, battle, or occasion. The celebration enables us to release pent-up stress from the previous "battle" and reenergizes us. The celebration gives us permission to see the old for what it was and motivates us to look ahead to what might be. Celebration is a part of the transformational process.

The Humbled Miriam

Years later Miriam appeared again in the narrative of Israel's forty-year sojourn through the desert. Though the nation had been freed from Egypt, their transformation into the people of God ready to possess their Promised Land took four decades and the raising up of another generation. (What a helpful reminder in our contemporary spiritual journeys that spiritual transformation is a life-long process!)

At one particularly challenging juncture of the wilderness wanderings, Moses' wife and sons from Midian joined him. Perhaps the presence of another woman in Moses' life prompted some jealousy in the protective older sister. Miriam had been the "first lady" as long as Zipporah was living in Midian. Once she was able to join her husband, Zipporah's entrance created tensions within the leadership team. Theories of group dynamics teach us that new members to a team create new dynamics that must be attended to. The team cannot assume that nothing has changed because what exists is, in essence, a totally new team that must experience its own developmental cycle and create its own identity, cohesiveness, and spirit.

So it was that when Zipporah joined Moses, both Miriam and her brother Aaron began to complain against Moses because of his wife (Numbers 12:1). They began to challenge the leadership of Moses, perhaps questioning his judgment—or what they considered lack of judgment—for marrying a woman of a different nation. (Isn't it amazing that two people who themselves had been discriminated against based on their ethnic identity, used ethnic differences as the basis for their dislike of the union between Zipporah and Moses?)

I wonder, however, if their challenge was really less about Zipporah's ethnicity—or even Moses' leadership—and more about their fears and feelings of inadequacy in leadership. Perhaps deep down they questioned their own significance, worth, and importance to the cause. The leadership team was in the midst of a desert, and it was taking years to go a distance that should have taken days. The wilderness experience must have been frustrating, and the people demanded a great deal from Moses as the central figure on the leadership team. For Aaron and Miriam, who were less visible than Moses, perhaps it was their pride or their frustration that caused them to question the authority and "anointing" of Moses: "Has the

Lord spoken only through Moses? Hasn't [God] also spoken through us?" (Numbers 12:2)

God called the leadership team together and confronted both Miriam and Aaron about the folly of attacking Moses. It is not clear why Miriam was struck with leprosy and Aaron was not. Perhaps it was because she was the eldest, or perhaps because she was the leader of the instigation. Perhaps it was because Aaron acknowledged their sin, crying out to Moses, ". . . do not hold against us the sin we have so foolishly committed" (Numbers 12:11), while Miriam did not immediately repent. Perhaps she needed time and space to reflect upon her actions.

When Moses interceded with God on her behalf, God imposed a seven-day banishment upon her, after which the leprosy would be cleared and she could return to the camp. It is important to note that, through all of this, the people of Israel did not move forward without Miriam, indicating her importance to the nation.

Being cast out from the camp must have been humiliating for Miriam, and from that experience she no doubt learned a deeper level of humility that enhanced her future leadership. As leaders we are human—sometimes all too human. Too often we want to share the victorious and celebratory moments of leadership and ignore the humbling experiences that point out our frail humanity. From Miriam we learn not only the importance of humility but also the reality of our humanity. Miriam was not perfect, nor were her brothers—Moses had murdered an Egyptian in a fitful rage and Aaron cowardly designed an idol to which the people bowed down in Moses' absence (Exodus 32:1-8). Yet God chose Miriam, Moses, and Aaron to lead the journey of transformation of God's people.

God calls some to preach and some to teach, some to oversee finances and some to direct business affairs, some to nurture and some to inspire—and some to dance. Each gift is important and each leader is important. At any given time, one leader may be at the forefront of a movement or cause—being specially endowed by God for that season. The rest of us must remain confident in our own gifts and prayerfully consider the purposes to which we have been called for that time and season.

The Choreography of Miriam

From watchful sister, to celebratory leader, to humbled servant, Miriam provides a picture of the development of a leader—with all of its twists and turns. Her role in the life of ancient Israel spanned almost a century, and her leadership illustrates her importance to the nation and her celebrated place on the leadership team that transformed a nation.

Miriam's dance took place at three distinct junctures of Israel's journey from Egypt to Canaan. In her early years, Miriam lived during a time of fear and oppression and her people waited on God for deliverance. Miriam's role was to set in motion the deliverance of the deliverer—the baby boy who would grow up to help lead the nation out of their bondage.

At a second juncture, when the Hebrews crossed over the Red Sea, thus escaping the threats of the Egyptians forever, Miriam's role was to help them recognize their transition from slaves to a fledgling nation by celebrating and commemorating what God had done and would continue to do in their lives.

At the third juncture, when the Hebrews were stuck in the wilderness—not willing to retreat back to Egypt, yet unable to move forward—Miriam's difficult lesson in humility demonstrated the necessity for a time of repentance. Her temporary banishment was a lesson for all that, after failure, it is possible to get up and move forward.

Miriam serves as a model to young girls and mature women alike that God can and will use each of us, in our own ways, at our own stages of development, to influence others in life-changing ways. Miriam's leadership is evidence of God's many ways of bringing key people together for transformative purposes and reminds us to take time to *celebrate* God's work in us. Miriam also reminds us that, though we may stumble in life's journey—and even miss a beat or two—through God's grace we can dance again.

Reflection and Discussion Questions

1. Think of women who have initiated celebrations in your life. What skills and qualities did they possess?

2. What was the most recent transition in your life? In what symbolic ways did you close out the old before moving to the new?

3. What was your most recent crisis? Did you create any space for celebration when you got through it? Did you take any time to laugh, sing, dance, rejoice? If not, what do you wish you might have done to celebrate the end of that time?

4. Do you help people who work for and with you to celebrate? What rituals do you use to celebrate accomplishments at work? In your church or community? In your family?

5. Miriam's story intimates that even after failure we can dance again. Can you think of a time in which you failed as a leader? In what ways were you able to reflect on and learn from this failure?

Chapter 5

The Leader as Choreographer

Different faith traditions view dancing in different ways. I grew up in the Holiness tradition, which taught that dancing to music was "worldly" and not pleasing to God. In this same church, though, we did the "holy dance" or shouted when the Spirit was high in our praise services.

During the slave era in the United States, women and men in the slave churches celebrated with the "ring-shout," a praise dance that can be traced back to West African traditions. On-looking white Christians often shuddered at these displays, considering the movements to be too sensuous or even animalistic. Some well-intentioned, yet misguided, missionaries taught that it was all right to do the holy dance or ring-shout as long as the dancer's legs never crossed, for then the movement signified something sinful.

Among the ancient Israelites, dancing was a symbol of joy, and women danced to celebrate joyous occasions (see Psalm 30:11; Ecclesiastes 3:4; Luke 15:25). Women generally participated in dancing either individually or in groups with other women. The Bible gives several other examples of dancing: groups of women dancing at celebrations of military victories (1 Samuel 18:6); maidens dancing at Shiloh, probably as part of a religious celebration (Judges 21:19–23); and children imitating the dance in their play (Job 21:11; Matthew 11:17).[1] Some scholars suggest that dancing was widespread in the ancient Near East and that choreography was highly developed in the ancient kingdoms of Judah and Israel.[2]

A series of Hebrew words for dance can be found in the Bible:

> *hagag*—"to dance in a circle"
> *savav*—"to encircle," "to turn about,
>   "to circuambulate"
> *raqad* and *pizzez*—"to skip"
> *qippes* and *dilleg*—"to jump"
> *kirker*—"to whirl," "to pirouette"
> *pasah*—"to limp"
> *hyl* or *hll*—"to perform a whirling dance"
> *siheq*—"to dance," "to play"[3]

According to the Amnon Shiloah in the *International Encyclopedia of Dance*, "the most frequently used Hebrew term for 'dance' is *mahol*, derived from the verbal root *hll* ('to whirl'); literally it means 'whirling.' "[4] It is significant that Miriam and the dancers led the Israel nation in *mahol* after their triumphant passage through the Sea (Exodus 15:20), indicating that they whirled ecstatically in celebration of their new-found freedom.

Dancing in scripture is often portrayed as a means of praising God, expressing joy, and celebrating freedom. I like how the editors of the *Dictionary of Biblical Imagery* describe dancing:

> Dancing, in its essence, is always symbolic. It is laughter, being pleasant; turning in a circle; whirling, running and leaping—an agile leaping

that becomes an artistic rhythmic body movement expressing feeling and thought. (p. 188)

Dr. James Gibson, author of *Healing Wisdom of the
Bible,* gives us another perspective on dancing:

When I speak of dancing, I do not mean only
dancing on a stage or at a party. Dancing need not
involve great physical exertion or long training in
a studio. We can dance in spirit. We can move
gracefully in all that we do. Our eyes and lips can
dance when we meet an old friend. Our hearts
and minds can dance when we see joy of a new
birth. Our souls can dance when we encounter
justice and compassion, or mercy and healing in
the world. We can move through our work and relationships with grace and charm. (p. 196)

Dr. Gibson describes David's dancing before
the ark and considers David's dance to be "a marvelous
image of the power and beauty of this ancient king's love
of God . . . for King David, dancing was a kind of prayer. It
was his way of communicating to God and his friends his
feelings and emotions" (p. 195).

Awesome is the leader who understands the
power of dance and celebration and optimistically leads
people through the movements of life. Choreographic
leaders are leaders who dance their vision of life, develop
dance routines that enable other people to dance the vision, translate the significance of the dance steps, and free
people to dance.

Dancing the Vision

Vision is crucial to transformative leadership. Not only does the leader as choreographer hold a vision of the transformative aims to which she will move people, but she also dances the vision in a way that invites others to join and internalize the vision for themselves. Vision for transformation often emerges out of everyday circumstances that need to be changed, and a significant role of the leader who wants to embrace a vision is to pay attention to the things around her.

One such woman of vision is Dr. Brenda Salter-McNeil, who is the President and Founder of Overflow Ministries International, an organization dedicated to raising up a generation of reconcilers. Overflow International hosts conferences, retreats, and training sessions that raise people's awareness of the ravaging effects of racism and ethnocentricity, and provides them with the knowledge and skills to counter these effects. Brenda envisions a multicultural church that reflects "every nation, tribe, people and language" worshipping before the throne of God (Revelation 7:9) and choreographs ways that help people move toward racial reconciliation and healing.

When she graduated from seminary and began working with a national campus ministry organization, she quickly realized that this ministry was not attracting black students. Identifying what it was that kept black students from joining this ministry led her into the dance of racial reconciliation, a dance to which she has now committed her life's work.

Brenda started by finding and identifying with African American students on campus and inviting them to become a part of the campus ministry. The initial obstacle was the fact that this organization had historically been comprised of and led by European American students and staff members, and its norms and practices reflected those of this majority culture. Initially, the African American students Brenda brought into the group felt out of place. But Brenda encouraged them to continue coming as she continued to dance the vision herself. She worked to include these newer students by affirming the gifts they possessed and reassuring them they had contributions to make.

As the vision continued to evolve for Brenda, she began a process that I call the "leadership shuffle"—moving between and dancing within two groups of people. This shuffle is critical to developing a shared vision, especially among diverse groups of people. Brenda exposed the black students to the worship styles of the white students, and she exposed the white students to the worship styles of the black students. She taught the leadership and older members of the ministry the "steps" that the newer African American students were more accustomed to dancing. She taught the black students the steps the ministry traditionally danced. Brenda developed a parallel leadership structure to help the black students who had leadership capacity but had been overlooked by the traditional structure, and she eventually found ways to integrate these two leadership structures. One thing became clear to Brenda very early: She knew that her vision entailed bringing together people of different backgrounds.

Though she was still learning the practical steps, Brenda became increasingly committed to the vision of racial reconciliation. When she joined the leadership of the regional staff of this campus ministry, she was one of a handful of black and Latino staff members working in a predominantly white ministry organization during an era when few people were successfully developing truly inter-ethnic ministry teams. The dance was a bit awkward at first, and they often stepped on each other's feet. There were times when staff members' stereotypical assumptions of each other led to insensitive remarks and innuendoes. There were times when decisions were made that did not reflect the needs of an increasingly diverse constituency. Yet Brenda kept dancing.

She and the handful of other staff members of color resisted the temptation to leave the organization and find a new dance floor. They also resisted the temptation to dance the steps expected of them. Brenda laughingly recalls, "It took a lot of bravery for me to be my loud, exuberant, Pentecostal self in an organization that was unfamiliar with such a charismatic style." Her willingness to persist in the dance, in her way, helped the organization change to accommodate a more complex, syncopated dance that encompassed the traditions and styles of many groups. The ministry events began to reflect elements of a number of cultural traditions, and, Brenda recalls, the ministry became more racially-reconciled than ever before.

This ministry "dance floor" upon which Brenda learned her dance of racial reconciliation, inspired the launching of Overflow International that became Brenda's primary stage for dancing and realizing her God-given vision.

Developing Dance Routines

In order to dance her vision, the choreographic leader must develop routines that enable others to participate in the dance. As leader of Overflow International, Brenda has developed a series of routines, based on her years of experience in racial reconciliation and work in cross-cultural contexts, that help people participate in the dance of racial reconciliation regardless of their level of familiarity or expertise.

The first step of her routine is to create an inter-ethnic leadership team of trainers and workers. For every ministry event that Overflow hosts, Brenda builds and maintains relationships with women and men of a variety of ethnic heritages—Latina, Asian American, European American, African American. She and her team literally embody the vision of a reconciling team committed to the vision of racial dance.

The second step of Brenda's ministry is to incorporate multiethnic worship. Brenda believes true racial reconciliation must start with the transformation of the heart, and worship opens our hearts to the spiritual truth of reconciliation. She views worship as the process of experiencing the presence of God and making an intimate acquaintance with God. She recognizes, however, that each of us experiences God in our own way and that people of different cultural backgrounds may engage God differently. Therefore, she creates worship services that are multiethnic, using music, liturgy, and rituals from a variety of cultural traditions. At any given event she might incorporate silence and singing, liturgy and literature, high praise and popular singing, or banners and dancing. She works to create an atmosphere that allows people to engage God in their own way, enabling them to participate in the dance of reconciliation in their own way. She is, at the same time, exposing people to a variety of cultural expressions, enabling them to appreciate each other's worship styles.

A fundamental step in Brenda's dance routine stems from her belief that reconciliation is based on biblical truths. Believing that God calls us to racial reconciliation and has given us revelation of this vision in the Bible, she includes a biblical teaching module about reconciliation in all of her conferences, retreats, and training sessions.

Perhaps at the core of Brenda's ability to choreograph dance routines is her ability to create space for people to share their stories. She uses what she calls "safe facilitation," giving people time and space to reflect on their own dance. Into each event, Brenda incorporates opportunities for participants to reflect on their stories and hear the stories of others. It is only in hearing each other's stories, she believes, that we can truly connect with each other's path and pain. It is from this point of interconnectedness that we can initiate the potential of reconciliation.

Showing the Significance of the Steps

Choreographers know that every dance step, every movement has meaning and is significant to the performance of the dance. So it is with the leader who will help people to dance a vision. She must be able to show her dancers the significance of the steps; she needs to help people to understand the meaning of these steps in their lives. Sister Thea Bowman was just such a choreographic leader.

Sister Thea Bowman was an African American Catholic nun who was a driving force behind the black Catholic movement of the 1970s and 1980s. As a teen, Thea attended Holy Child Catholic School, a high school run by the Franciscan Sisters of Perpetual Adoration. She was so moved by the social justice work of these Catholic brothers and sisters that she wanted to join them in feeding the hungry, helping the homeless, and educating children.[5] In 1953 Thea entered the Franciscan Sisters' community in LaCrosse, Wisconsin, where she remained for eight years before moving back to Canton, Mississippi, to teach English and music at the high school she attended in her youth.

In her video autobiography entitled *Sr. Thea: Her Own Story,* Thea talks about those early days in the Franciscan community. She studied and helped to build community but was very conscious of being black in a white order. Later, other members of the community acknowledged that living with a black person had been new for them, and in many ways they tried to shape Thea into one of them, to be just like them.

But Thea had a strong sense of who she was, of her gifts and identity cultivated in the bosom of black culture. Out of this intense appreciation and sense of awareness, she became a pioneer in bringing black culture to the Catholic church and an early trailblazer of the black Catholic movement. Sister Thea had a vision of an inclusive church where various cultural traditions could be freely expressed. Her mission was to show the world and the church what it meant to be both black and Catholic. Father Michael Pfleger, priest of the Community of St. Sabina, a black Catholic church in Chicago, said of her, "Sister Thea came to put the African American plate on the menu. She came to bring the expressions of the church to its fullness. She brought joy and her music was a way for her to loosen up all people."[6]

As a leader, Thea broke barriers. She played a vital role in the Institute for Black Catholic Studies at Xavier University that trained primarily white seminarians about black experience, expressions, and culture. When commenting on her leadership, Father Pfleger said, "Without Thea as choreographer . . . too many people across the world would have failed to grasp the import of the black Catholic reality. Without the steps, what they were being taught would have been just information. Sister Thea embodied the movement, the grace, and the joy of God's people."[7]

Those who knew her well insist that Sister Thea's dance came from the heart. She maintained a joy and spirituality that invigorated everything she did. Her dance for life came from a heart full of love and compassion for people—the mark of any leader who will transform others.

In 1984 Thea was diagnosed with cancer, and both her parents died in the same year. Her intense faith served as the wellspring from which she garnered strength during this trying time. As her sickness progressed, she found that "her illness became her entrance."[8] As a powerful black woman in the prime of life, some leaders within the church had perceived Thea as a threat. But confined to a wheelchair during her long illness, Thea was received with openness and could reach those whom she could not reach standing up. In her wheelchair her spirit continued to dance.

In 1989 Thea was invited to speak at the Meeting of the National Conference of U.S. Bishops, a profound honor and opportunity for her. Later, when reflecting on this momentous occasion, Sister Marie Augusta Neal made the comment, "She made the bishops dance."[9] During that address to the bishops, Sister Thea spoke from the depths of her heart about the vision to which she had been drawn for most of her life: "Today we are called to walk together in a new way to that land of promise, to celebrate who we are and whose we are." She continued to call the leaders of the church to the real challenge of walking together in unity, to resist the traditional divisions that separate the church by laity and clergy, by gender and race.

"The church teaches us that the church is a family, a family of families, and the family has to stay together. And we know that if we do stay together, if we walk and talk and work and play and stand together in Jesus' name, we'll be who we say we are, truly catholic and we shall overcome. Overcome the poverty, the loneliness, the alienation and build together a holy city, a New Jerusalem, a city set apart where they'll know we're His because we love one another."[10]

The bishops were captivated. One bishop recalled how Sister Thea "electrified the bishops of the United States . . . She expressed so beautifully the history of the black Catholic church in the United States. We've seen other faces of it, but I think [she] was the authentic face—a face of reconciling love—a face that did not in any way minimize the difficulties, the pain. It was just a profoundly moving thing, and I had a sense of deep gratitude to God that this was happening."[11]

As Sister Thea finished her speech, she spontaneously broke into the chorus of the song that had become the hallmark of the Civil Rights Movement, "We Shall Overcome." Her strong melodious voice bellowed out and the bishops joined her. After the first chorus, she stopped singing momentarily and called out, "Ya'll get up." First one, then two and three, then the entire audience of bishops stood to their feet.

Three bishops had been seated near her on the stage. They likewise stood and gathered around her as she reached for their hands, her arms crossed at her forearms.

She proceeded to teach the bishops the steps to the unity "dance"—the swaying back and forth to the music, hand and arms interlocked. As she modeled the posture from the podium with the clergy leaders on the stage, she instructed, "Cross your right hand over your left hand." Some hesitated. She gently chided in the manner of black "signifying": "You've got to move together to do that. You've got to move together with me." Thea was leading a movement of the heart from her wheelchair.

The audience laughed, and she continued to teach the significance of the steps they were now marking out. "See, in the old days you had to tighten up so that when the bullets would come, so that when the tear gas would come, when the dogs would come, when the forces would come, when the tanks would come, brothers and sisters would not be separated." Thea then injected a lesson on leading by example in addressing worldwide struggles: "You remember where they put the clergy and bishops in those old days? Right up in front to lead the people in solidarity with our brothers and sisters in the church who suffer in South Africa, who suffer in Poland, who suffer in Ireland, in Nicaragua, that suffer in Northern Ireland, who suffer all over the world." Then she shifted to a new chorus, "We shall live in love, we shall live in love, we shall live in love, today." They sang. They held hands, arm in arm, and the bishops began to sway to the music in the tradition of the black church as Sister Thea led them in song and in an experience of solidarity.[12] Together they danced Sister Thea's God-given vision.

Freeing People to Dance

After the transformative leader choreographs the movements of her vision and teaches the significance of the steps of her dance, she must then help people experience the freedom to actually *dance*. The dance ministry of Thera Ward provides a few insights on freeing people to dance. She believes that we can express certain truths through dance and movement more powerfully than we can through words, and her vision is to establish dance ministries throughout the country.

Thera is a professionally trained dancer who has danced on Broadway and in the Dance Theater of Harlem. Tall, svelte, and assured, Thera is continually amazed that she is actually leading a dance ministry. She never saw herself as a leader but now realizes she was in preparation for leading this dance ministry during her entire twenty-one-year professional dance career.

When women first come to join Thera's dance ministry, she has them complete a written questionnaire, giving their views on dance and ministry and describing how they feel about themselves. This tool helps her discern these potential dancers' perspectives and mindsets that will either facilitate or hinder their movement as dancers. Not surprisingly, Thera has observed that women who are comfortable with their body size and shape move more freely than those who disdain their bodies. She has also learned what every effective leader comes to appreciate: pessimistic or negative thinking patterns and mindsets are often the key barriers to people's success and effectiveness. The leader must help people develop perspectives and paradigms that will reinforce success, not failure.

Thera starts with potential dancers by helping them get comfortable, teaching them to trust their senses, their movements, and the movements of the other dancers. Before she teaches any new skills or dance steps, she teaches her dancers to listen carefully to the music and to the rhythms of the music, to observe what is going on around them.

She often starts new people with dancing in silence, just moving their legs and arms. Then she has them begin simple movements, basic steps, and dance positions, gradually moving out a little, then a little more. While teaching new steps, she also teaches about mental blocks and emotional mountains that can prevent them from dancing freely. She designs space for group prayer time and group interaction to help each dancer push through the mountains that might block her movements. Thera believes that a person cannot dance without being free, and she views dancing as a way for people to let down their guard and be open to the moving of the Spirit.

As the new dancers master basic steps and get more comfortable with Thera and with each other, she begins to see their countenances and confidence levels change. She has watched many a dancer begin with a cowering demeanor and open up, moving confidently and gracefully. She has seen their movement turn from a dance of pain to a dance of liberty.

So it is that the leader as choreographer helps free people to dance. Regardless of the stage—the corporate arena, the community agency, the neighborhood group—leaders who truly have a transformative effect on the lives of people help people move past barriers to a place where they can freely dance their dance. Effective corporate leaders have learned this vital lesson of leadership: It is their job to remove things that serve as barriers to their people's effective performance. These barriers might be poor working conditions, lack of research and development funds, lack of technology or minimal skills for using new technology. These leaders still expect their people to perform and hold them accountable for performance, but they realize unless the stage is cleared, their people may never perform up to their true potential.

Effective choreographic leaders spend time walking with the people they lead. Only then can they help people remove the barriers that block their movement and help free them from inhibitions and doubts. Too often a vision of change and transformation scares people. They cannot imagine dancing the new vision. They get stage fright, and they fear falling on their faces. Sometimes they have never danced this dance before; sometimes they just fear the unknown. The choreographic leader creates space that enables people in her troupe or team or business to experiment—to start with small steps and gradually build up their confidence to try more difficult routines. Ultimately, the choreographer understands the power of dance in the work of transformation and understands her role in helping experience fullness of freedom to move forward.

The Choreography of Leadership

Leaders such as Brenda, Sister Thea, and Thera Ward are choreographers who transform the independent actions of individuals into a collective, orchestrated, purposeful movement. It takes a special kind of leadership to synchronize the activities and rhythms of individuals.

From Brenda's dance of racial reconciliation, we learn that the choreographer holds a vision vivid enough not only to dance it herself, but compelling enough to choreograph it so that others might also perform it.

From Sister Thea's vision of a church unified and connected, not fragmented by status, class, or race, we see how the leader as choreographer can share her vision of the possibilities by helping others learn the significance of the steps.

From Thera's teaching, we understand the choreographer's importance in helping people see old things in new ways, in motivating individuals to overcome hurdles, and freeing people to move, both literally and figuratively.

The true choreographic leader is moved from her heart and moves the heart of others. She moves to the rhythm of the Spirit, inspiring people to new levels of faith and effectiveness as they celebrate life.

Some of you are in situations that require you to communicate a vision or ideal in ways in which words alone cannot adequately express its strength. In these situations actions do speak louder than words, and perhaps you can create dance routines that help people embrace your vision.

Some of you have been called to rally people around a cause, and you need to choreograph a march, a parade, or some other event that brings your issues to the public's attention.

Some of you have been called to advance ideological purposes, such as peace, respect, freedom, or safety. Nonverbal means may help you convey the essence and importance of your vision and help people see what these lofty ideals look like and how they might be put into concrete action.

Some of you play a significant role in helping others experience the joy of life. Without your leadership, they might give up. You may have been called to help create conditions in which others can freely offer their gifts and talents.

Some of you have been called to bring people of diverse backgrounds and interests together, and it will be as a choreographer that you will help synchronize their plans and steps.

Pray about and consider the needs and applications to which you can choreograph your leaders.

Reflection and Discussion Questions

1. Do you know someone who is dancing her vision? How does she get others to share or dance the vision with her?

2. In what ways do you see yourself as a choreographic leader? When and how do you bring people together for a collective purpose? What "dance routines" are important to you?

3. As you look around you, in your home, your neighborhood, your workplace, what are some things that need to be changed for the better? What vision of this change could you "dance" or share with others?

4. Reflect on anything that might be blocking your ability to dance freely. What are ways that you might be able to reduce these barriers to your dance?

5. How might you invite others to join you in your dance? What are some things that might limit or prevent them from joining you in this dance? What are some things you could do to encourage them?

The Leader as Weaver

Chapter 6

Deborah—The Relational Leader*

History is filled with women leaders who have fought passionately for social causes of equality, freedom, and justice. Women such as Elizabeth Cady Stanton, Susan B. Anthony, and Sojourner Truth believed that women could never be free without equal voice in the political process, and they worked passionately and strategically to elevate the issue of voting rights to the public consciousness. A leading lady from antiquity, a judge named Deborah, also fought passionately for the liberation of her people from oppressive conditions. Her leadership is instructive for us today, as we try to make sense out of senseless injustices and work collaboratively for justice.

A Woman of Fire

In order to understand Deborah's leadership, we need to know the history of her people. After the death of Moses, the people of Israel had reclaimed the land they believed God had promised them. For the next two hundred years, they lived in a cycle of freedom and oppression in which ongoing conflict and skirmishes between various tribal colonies of Israel and its neighbors were common. Even in times of extended peace, the Israelites had to remain vigilant to ward off raiders and threats. When they re-

---

* *The account of Deborah's leadership can be found in Judges 4-5.*

mained spiritually and morally strong, they were able to protect their communities and remain independent.

There were other times when Israel's priorities changed. The writer of Judges declared, "The Israelites did evil in the sight of the Lord" (Judges 3:7, 4:1). Losing sight of God's vision left them vulnerable to attacks by their marauding enemies. Their weakened spiritual condition and their fragmentation made the community easily penetrable and open to antagonistic military force.

When they found they could not fight off or protect themselves, in desperation they cried out to God for help. The external threats served as a wake up call to unite, but they still needed a force around which they could rally to unify their goals.

The writer of Judges explains the divine intervention that broke the oppressive hold on the people: "Then the Lord raised up judges who saved them out of the hands of these raiders" (Judges 2:16). Of the twelve judges chronicled in the Book of Judges, at least six were responsible for military leadership, while others maintained political and administrative leadership. These judges organized the people, settled disputes, built up the community, and rallied the people to fight their oppressors.

Of the twelve judges recorded, Deborah is the only identified woman. Her story is told in two forms: in narrative form (Judges 4) and in poetic form (Judges 5). It is Deborah's poem, or song, that gives insight into the sad conditions that called forth her leadership. For twenty agonizing years, the people of Israel had been oppressed by the military presence of a neighboring ruler named Jabin. The commander of Jabin's army, Sisera, had led the occupation and most likely coercively enforced restrictive laws and policies. His battalion of nine hundred chariots posed an intimidating force, and it was into this situation that Deborah walked boldly as both prophetess and judge.

Not only is the fact of Deborah's leadership significant, but also her style. She is said to have been the "wife of Lappidoth" (Judges 4:4), which some scholars translate as "woman of fire."[1] Indeed Deborah was a courageous woman and a passionate leader, a woman of fire.

A Leader in Touch with Her People

As an established "sitting" judge, Deborah held court under the Palm of Deborah located between two cities, Ramah and Bethel in the hill country. Like the weaver who dedicates space for her art, Deborah carved out space in which the people could come to have their disputes settled. A later judge, Samuel, used more of an itinerant style, annually traveling the circuit of towns to reach the people and settle their spiritual problems (I Samuel 7:16). While neither style is better than the other, I wonder if establishing a space for interaction and problem solving is a lesson we can credit to Deborah's female brand of leadership. People need a safe place in which to share their stories—a space for emotional, as well as physical safety. As leaders carve out safe space, people are able and willing to establish trusting relationships and share their concerns and cares, dreams and fears.

The people in this border region trusted Deborah's judicious wisdom because she genuinely heard their disputes. Powerful is the leader who can listen closely to people to understand their deepest needs. Deborah was a leader who was in touch with the needs of her people and the conditions in which they lived. As people came to her, each bringing their own strand of misery and hopelessness, their stories might have seemed unconnected to the untrained eye. But just as a weaver discerns the pattern of a frayed and tattered cloth, Deborah saw the effects of the forces that were rending the fabric of her society. It takes a wise leader to discern the broader issues and make connections, and Deborah could see that the power of the occupying forces that had created oppressive conditions for her people had to be broken.

It is significant that Deborah described herself as "a mother in Israel" (Judges 5:7). Whether she was speaking literally or figuratively, rarely do we see "mother" as symbolic with leader. (Most often we hear about our "founding fathers"!) Yet here we see Deborah as both mother and leader, as listener, encourager, perhaps even nurturer—qualities traditionally associated with women but not with strong leaders.

A Leader Who Understands the Issues

Whatever disputes the people brought to her, Deborah no doubt was more troubled by the bigger conflict she saw: Her land was occupied; the people of her land were not free. Settling their conflicts with each other was of little consequence if the conflict with the occupier was not addressed.

Deborah's words in Judges 5:6-8 describe the oppressive conditions under which the people had lived for twenty long years under the domination of Jabin. The first issue Deborah grasped was that "war came to the city gates" (Judges 5:8). When violence and danger come to the gates of a community, the community has no safety and security. In this case, the enemy had crept in, and the people were living in occupied territory. Perhaps the pressure of this external conflict also increased their internal conflict and their disputes with each other.

Deborah's song also tells us that the "roads were abandoned" and "travelers took winding paths" (Judges 5:6). To avoid the occupied military forces, people of the community could not walk the main streets and resorted to traveling on back roads. Unfortunately, traveling back roads brings its own risks and set of dangers. If the main thoroughfares were blocked or rendered inaccessible, the primary trade routes would also be impeded, leaving the community with little or no economic security.

Deborah portrays the grim reality of everyday life: "village life in Israel ceased" (Judges 5:7). In other words, the sense of community that comes with lively public meetings in the thoroughfares and marketplaces had been destroyed; the people experienced no sense of togetherness. Deborah also notes that the people "chose new gods"(Judges 5:8), suggesting that under these harsh conditions, people had forsaken the religious tradition that had both identified and strengthened them as a people. They were losing their identity, moral strength, and their hope.

Even worse, the people seemed to have lost their will to defend and fight for their community. Deborah reported, "not a shield or spear was seen among forty thousand in Israel" (Judges 5:8). The region seemed to be wallowing in despair and apathy. It was time for somebody to take the lead! God raised up Deborah as just that leader, giving her a brilliant strategy for overthrowing the oppressive forces that held her people in gridlock.

A Leader Who Partners

When Deborah heard from God, receiving a plan for change and transformation, she went directly to Barak, the military leader of a neighboring community. She knew she needed a general to recruit and deploy the military forces necessary in order to execute God's plan. Identifying and building a strong military team was critical to her strategy.[2] Deborah told Barak that he was to mobilize the troops from the communities of Naphtali and Zebulon and that God would create battle conditions ensuring victory. "God," Deborah assured Barak, "will lure Sisera into your hands" (Judges 4:7).

Barak, however, was not sold on this unconventional battle plan. He was not convinced that he was the hero of the hour and was unwilling to risk his troops without more assurance. So what does a leader do when she sees a solution, but those needed to implement it do not see it quite the same way? She listens. She listens to what the people are saying, and she hears their concerns.

Barak answered Deborah with this bargain: "If you go with me, I will go; but if you don't go with me, I won't go" (Judges 4:8). Perhaps Barak was concerned about the efficacy of Deborah's plan and needed assurance of God's hand in it. Perhaps he argued that if this plan were truly God's will, the prophetess of God would surely accompany him into battle.

Whatever his reasons, Deborah listened and agreed to accompany him into battle. In doing so, she demonstrated her willingness to partner with another leader to accomplish the greater cause. Deborah became a weaver of a relationship that would be vital to carrying out God's plan: Deborah brought spiritual power and Barak brought military might. Together they would fight to free their people from the occupying forces.

The two of them proceeded to Kedesh, where Barak put forth a call for volunteer fighters. Deborah's leadership had a ripple effect. Initially people from Barak's hometown enlisted, and as Deborah and Barak influenced this key group of "princes" (Judges 5:2) to respond to the crisis. They in turn influenced people from the neighboring communities of Ephraim, Benjamin, Makir, Zebulun, and Issacher to join the growing army. In all, ten thousand troops prepared for battle.

In the meantime Sisera, too, was gathering his fighters together and marching them from a place called Harosheth Haggoyim (Judges 4:13) to the Kishon River. Prophetically, Deborah sensed it was the time to proceed to battle, and she gave the rallying cry: "Go! This is the day the Lord has given Sisera into your hands. Has not the Lord gone ahead of you?" (Judges 4:14). As Barak led the military charge down Mount Tabor, Deborah led the spiritual charge. Barak sharpened their battle plan, and Deborah lifted their spirits. Encouraging herself so she could encourage the troops—"Oh my soul, march on in strength" (Judges 5:21, NKJV)—leader Deborah walked with them into battle.

Picture this scene in your mind's eye: During this time of the year, the Kishon River valley was extremely muddy. As Sisera's army came charging across the plain, their heavy chariots started getting stuck in the muddy valley. With Barak's troops bearing down on them, Sisera was forced to abandon his chariot to escape the onslaught. After that, it probably did not take much for Barak to pursue and conquer the rest of the troops.

The bottom line was this: With Sisera and the troops gone, Jabin the Canaanite king had no more power. The Israelites were free! With the threat to the community gone, Deborah's vision could become a reality. As judge and leader, Deborah could work with the community to mend the ruptured seams of their society. Strands of safety, economic security, visionary and collaborative leadership could be interlaced to create a durable community.

A Leader Who Praises

Deborah's song of praise to God for the liberation of her people gives us additional insight into her leadership. She knew that it was only under the providence of God that she and her military team could have put up such a valiant fight. In fact Deborah intimates that not only did the God of heaven fight for Israel, but the stars of heaven joined in the battle to overthrow Sisera (Judges 5:20).

Deborah also honored the princes who took the lead and served as catalysts for more people to join the cause. Deborah's homage to the leaders of battle reminds us of the importance of acknowledging those men and women who work with us and who play a crucial role in meeting our mutual objectives. The leader who is rich in praises is a leader who realizes the importance of people to the leadership equation.

Deborah also reminds us that things happen when leaders lead: people join the leadership team, people follow, and change occurs. According to Judges 4:24, the hand of the children of Israel grew stronger and stronger. Under passionate and united leadership, the people of the region were able to rebuild their community and live in peace for forty years.

The Strategic Weaver

Deborah was ultimately a weaver of relationships. As people came to bring their cases to her, she established their trust and built a relationship upon which they could rely, even in such times of uncertainty. They learned to trust her judgments, and eventually her challenges.

Her relationship-building skill was also critical to her effective partnering with Barak. To accomplish the strategic plan God had given her, Deborah knew she could not do it alone. Even though God had charged Barak to lead the military campaign, it took both Deborah and Barak to knit together the ten thousand troops necessary to enter into the battle that God had proclaimed would be won. It is also significant that Deborah accompanied Barak into battle, showing her continued weaving of their relationship.

Deborah's leadership portrays another important quality of the leader as weaver: She could envision a tapestry of hope for the future that other people, living under the same hopeless conditions, could not yet see. Such vision is critical to transformative leadership. The leader who receives and acts upon a God-given strategy to move people toward the vision of transformation is the leader who leads in the footsteps of Deborah.

As a weaver adept at transforming unconnected bare threads into fine cloth, Deborah transformed a community that was falling apart, tearing at the seams, into a place of peace, ready for a new generation of God's people. Deborah, with God's guidance, saw beyond the seemingly disconnected complaints and disputes to the real issues of the day. Her challenge was to weave together the right people with the right actions to carry out the strategic plan God had spoken into her spirit. Her challenge was to hold the vision of a brighter day—a revitalized community. The image of that future community had to have been embroidered in her mind as she rallied Barak and the troops. This vision had the power to sustain and invigorate her.

Though our challenge as leading ladies differs from Deborah's military warfare, we, too, need to listen to the voices of those around us. We, too, need passion and conviction to help people make sense out of oppressive conditions. We, too, need to be able to envision a future tapestry that is better than the current one. And we may especially need to partner with others who can help us transform the future—we cannot do it alone.

Reflection and Discussion Questions

1. Who can you think of who creates a comfortable place in which to listen to people? How does she do this? How might you carve out more time and space to really listen to the people for whom you provide leadership?

2. Do you know someone who leads via partnership? How does she build relationships with other people? What ideas does this give you for creating partnerships on your own projects?

3. How do you handle people who don't want to collaborate or partner? How might you help them see the value of partnering to achieve goals? What alternative plans might you consider when you run into resistance with building partnerships?

4. When was the last time you praised those with whom you work? Members of your family? Fellow committee members? Think of some ways you could acknowledge their contribution to your mutual goals.

5. Can you think of a situation where you were able to see the "big picture" beyond the day-to-day obstacles? What helped you hold onto this vision? How did holding onto the vision help you get through the daily tasks?

Chapter 7

The Leader as Weaver

Weaving is one of the most ancient crafts and is known to have existed in many early cultures. In ancient Mesopotamia, North Africa, Nigeria, Ghana, India, and among the indigenous peoples of the Americas, people—often, but not always, women—practiced weaving for domestic, ritual, and commercial purposes.[1] Basket-making, embroidering, tapestry-making, tent-making, and weaving were all occupations and trades mentioned or referenced in biblical times. In Proverbs 31, we get a glimpse into the life of a nameless woman who was skilled at weaving. She is described as having nimble fingers and steady hands, and we are told she designed garments, produced them on her loom, and confidently negotiated with merchants for fair market value of her merchandise. The timeless art of interlacing thread, yarn, and other nature fibers into fine quality cloth, artful robes, intricate rugs, pillows, tent curtains, blankets, wall coverings, and shawls stands as testament to the creativity, vision, and skill of weavers throughout the ages.

Just as the weaver starts with an idea for a product for her household, or for a product that can be traded in the marketplace, the leader, too, starts with an idea or vision. A skillful weaver-leader can start with a dream, and weave together the necessary people and tasks to produce a product, an enterprise, or a service. Her raw materials are strands of ideas, needs, motivations, and aspirations that she deftly collects and laces together into a larger plan. By listening to the needs and desires of people, and by keeping her eye on the larger issues, or pattern, the weaver as leader can braid a pattern that enables others to see a vision more clearly and can move people toward collective goals.

Patterns of Weaving

Just as a weaver interlaces the warp and filling yarns,[2] the weaver-leader connects people with tasks and activities to produce the tapestry of the vision. The manner in which people and tasks are pulled together determines the type and effectiveness of her leadership. As the textile weaver must have a keen knowledge of her raw materials and the environment, so too the weaver-leader must have an understanding of the people with whom she will work, as well as the conditions in which they live.

Like the warp and the filling, the relationship between the leader and her people are the fibers of the leadership pattern. The type of weave—the style of leadership—is determined by the manner in which the yarns are interlaced. The leader who controls the activities develops a leadership pattern that is *directive*. This pattern or weave may be necessary for situations in which people need specific directions, where the tasks are simple, and when time is limited. People, however, may not grow and acquire their own leadership skills under this type of directive leadership pattern.

The *collaborative* leader, on the other hand, recognizes that she needs the commitment and skills of a variety of people to reach the goal. Rather than give instructions,

the collaborative leader uses her God-given empathy to ac-
tively listen to the expressed needs, desires, or discontent
of people in order to understand the tasks that need to be
completed. This type of leadership may be especially helpful when the group of people is larger and the tasks more
complex. People working within the collaborative leadership pattern will have more opportunity to offer their gifts
and grow as a result of the process.

The following comparison summarizes these two
patterns of leadership:

LEADERSHIP PATTERNS

DIRECTIVE	COLLABORATIVE
• Envisions an outcome or future that is better than the current one. The leader shares her vision and seeks the commitment and participation of others in her vision.	• Partially envisions an outcome or future that is better than the current one and continues to let the vision emerge as she taps into the needs, aspirations, and dreams of people.
• Determines the activities, tasks, and milestones necessary for the final outcome.	• Enlists other leaders and experts to determine the activities, tasks, and milestones necessary to realize the vision.
• Hires, selects appropriate people, and assigns them to the necessary tasks.	• Presents the activities and tasks and gives people an opportunity to assume the roles they feel most qualified to fulfill.
• Instructs people in how to accomplish the task.	
• Measures the results of the work and determines when the desired outcome has been achieved.	• Invites people to use their gifts, skills, and abilities and help to determine the best way to accomplish the task.

Skillful is the leader who can weave the pattern that enables others to see a vision more clearly. Whether directive or collaborative, the strength of the weaver is her ability to use the appropriate style at the appropriate time to transform a vision into reality.

Creating Space for a Vision to Develop

Often starting with nothing but raw ideas, the leader-weaver envisions a better future and then brings the right people together to transform "nothing" into "something," thought into action. The leader as weaver creates patterns and processes by which people can move forward. As a transformative leader, the weaver knows that the gift of creativity comes from the Creator, the vision for transformation from the heart of God.

One of the skills of the weaver-leader is her ability to tap into the spiritual power of creativity and envision something that does not yet exist. In the Genesis description of creation, we are told that, before God spoke, the earth was "formless and empty, darkness was over the surface of the deep." As "the Spirit of God was hovering over the waters," God spoke the world into existence (Genesis 1:2).

Think, for a moment, about this idea of "hovering." The essence of the Hebrew word *râchaph*, from which hovering derives, is similar to the idea of brooding[3]—the kind of brooding a mother hen does over her eggs. Her body provides warmth and creates an environment in which the baby chicks can develop, grow, and eventually hatch, full of life. Just as the Spirit of God hovered over the primordial waters, preparing the waters to bring forth life, the transformative leader must be still and allow the Spirit of God to hover over her unformed or pre-formed ideas and thoughts, and wait for the light of inspiration.

Different women engage in the "hovering" process differently. Some carve out time each morning for prayer, meditation, and devotions. Some pray specifically for clarity of thought on projects and products and keep track of their ideas in journals and notebooks. One such leading lady—a Deborah of *our* time—is Debra J. Collins, president and founder of Jurare Resource Group, a company that provides conference planning, training, and development. Debra considers "hovering time" vital to her leadership. In her house she has set aside a space where she goes to get quiet, pray, and meditate over ideas. This space has become associated with creativity for her.

She has also come to understand her times or cycles of creativity. For Debra, first thing in the morning or late at night seems to be the time when her creative juices flow and her ideas come most clearly. And she has trained herself to be sensitive to the voice of the Creator so that, whenever creative ideas come to mind, she stops a moment to capture the ideas on paper.

Debra's clients come to her with their visions for large-scale events, and she sees her job as weaver-leader to help bring their visions into reality. But she has also learned that oftentimes her clients cannot fully articulate their visions. She is careful to create space where they can express themselves and to provide enough time so that she can listen carefully to what they want. By questioning, probing, and listening, Debra interprets her client's vision on paper, transcribing, weaving their ideas into a clearly worded working document that becomes the "fabric" for achieving their goals.

Helping People Believe
They Can Achieve the Vision

Having a vision of a better future is not enough. The leader-weaver must be able to inspire others to move toward that vision. Helen Crawley, a director in a telecommunications company, excels at helping people embrace a new vision. She worked for a company that wanted to become a premier business communications network provider. Her mission was to develop wireless communication products and services for their clients. Before the proliferation of cell phones, her company was not a major player in the wireless division of the business. In fact, Helen started with zero team members and only one potential customer. Her biggest challenge was getting people to believe they *could* achieve the vision—and she understood that a leader must believe in the vision herself before she can inspire others to believe.

Helen's task was awesome. At each phase of the project, from building the team to working with customers, Helen had to face her own fears and trust God, claiming for herself the words spoken to a much earlier leader: "Be strong and courageous, because you will lead these people . . . do not be terrified; do not be discouraged, for the Lord your God will be with you wherever you go" (Joshua 1:6-9).

Developing a Strategy

Once a vision is clear to the people involved, the leader must weave together a strategy, a comprehensive plan, for bringing it to life. The weaver-leader understands that there is a gap between where people currently exist and where they will be once the vision is realized. She needs to develop a plan—either through directive or collaborative measures—to move people from where they are now to where they will be.

Helen's strategy for moving her organization into the wireless telephone business spanned three major areas: to develop quality software, to develop new testing and review processes, and to build strong customer relations. For each area, she built a team of people and collaboratively they developed plans, goals, and timelines for every project. Then in a more directive style, she set objectives for each manager and held each manager accountable for results. Eventually Helen ended up with eight technical managers reporting to her, five of whom managed multiple project teams. Altogether, Helen's staff managed fifteen projects simultaneously, with Helen as the weaver who braided people and tasks together. Each strategic focus area became the fibers that created the fabric of success.

Praising Progress

Large projects, campaigns—even dreams—can easily get bogged down in the details. The troops can get discouraged. The effective weaver-leader understands her role in helping people sustain the vision, and the importance of praise in motivating people to move forward. To acknowledge her teams for their hard work and progress, Helen started by translating broad strategy into specific goal statements. For instance, to become the premier provider of business communication networks meant they needed to provide high quality networks in shorter timeframes than their competitors. In a collaborative effort Helen and her team set goals for the *level* of quality they wanted from their vendors, the *number* of customers they wanted to obtain, and the *amount* of revenue they wanted to earn.

Next, Helen used a variety of communication vehicles to keep everyone aware of the progress and the goal. She posted "thermometer charts" showing current revenue at the bulb of the thermometer, with revenue goals indicated as the temperature gauge. Even though this might seem like a simple device, her charts helped teams track their progress and keep the goal visually in mind. Helen also started a newsletter in which she cited new customers, putting faces on the vision and sharing the stories behind the vision. She also gave presentations in every department to recognize progress. Helen committed to keeping the "big picture" personal and real for every person involved.

Connecting People and Tasks

The effective weaver-leader understands that each team member has different strengths and unique skills. There is a leading lady named Margaret Birt, president of PHD WallCoverings, who knows firsthand the value of matching people and tasks. For sixteen years Margaret has been helping customers transform ordinary rooms into extraordinary living spaces. It started when she was given an opportunity to buy a wallpapering business from a woman whom she had never met but who had heard about the quality of her freelance work. As a single mother raising three preteen children, Margaret had been praying for something to come into her life that would enable her to make a living and still spend time with her family. With nothing but a diamond ring for collateral, she took a leap of faith and bought the business.

Through the years, Margaret has expertly woven a network of craftspeople—including two of her now-adult children—to provide high quality service for customers. One of Margaret's key strengths is her ability to pull together the right team of people to collaboratively accomplish the job. There are times when one person can service a customer, but for large residential jobs, for commercial jobs or jobs that require painting and papering in high places, she creates crews where each person has a job in which they can flourish.

Margaret proudly described her team to me: Pat loves working with the more difficult, specialty paper. Her son, Andrew, is an excellent painter and is meticulous, and Margaret sends him to prep the walls for papering, aware that he always he leaves the place in perfect shape. Her daughter, Eileen, is a good businessperson whose customer interaction skills are superb. Eileen is also an artistic painter who specializes in faux finishes—a highly sought after look. Joanne, Margaret's sister, does whatever it takes to get a job done from start to finish. Joanne is dependable and leaves a job spic 'n' span. Rose, a new crew member, is an overall "Jill-of-all-trades" who helps with stripping paper, painting, and small carpentry jobs. On special jobs Margaret brings her mother on board, whom she fondly refers to as "eagle eyes" because her mother meticulously cuts strips of paper and catches any glitches in quality. Margaret understands that the secret to her success lies in the people on her team. Each team member has a specific skill, and together the entire team accomplishes its goal—with Margaret as the weaver who pulls them together.

Willing to Weave

Debra, Helen, and Margaret are all weavers who clarified their own, or another person's, vision. Like Habakkuk, they had the skill to "write the vision" (Habakkuk 2:2, KJV) so that others could see it and run with it.

They each understood that they could not actualize their vision alone. Each sought a team of people to carry out the strategic plan. Each carefully and wisely identified the tasks needed to achieve the goal and delegated these tasks to the appropriate people. Wisely, they sought people who had different skills than they did, rather than looking for people just like themselves. The weaver-leader understands the strength of the team is in its diversity of gifts, skills, and perspectives.

Many of you reading this book have visions and dreams of creating new enterprises, services, or products. Perhaps you face daunting tasks that seem overwhelming. Ask yourself: Whose help and support do I need to make this vision a reality? To whom do I need to listen to understand the issues? With whom might I want to partner? Where can I create some space and time where the Spirit can hover?

Your challenge is to be willing to weave when the opportunities for weaving present themselves.

Some of you are in organizations that are not very organized and could benefit from the touch of a skillful weaver.

Some of you know people in your organization who could make valuable contributions to a team, if only given opportunity to use their skills on the right assignment.

Some of your have been called to weave a new ministry or service. You have discerned a need and have a vision for meeting the need through a product or service. Perhaps your role is to prayerfully weave a plan and a team of people together to meet this need.

Pray about and consider where you can weave your God-given dream.

Reflection and Discussion Questions

1. Do you know someone in your life who leads by
    weaving? How does she bring people together?

2. In what ways do you weave threads of life together
    to make something happen?

3. Think of a time in your life when you had a vision
    for something and tried to enlist others to believe in
    your dream. What leadership pattern did you use,
    directive or collaborative? How effective was your
    style? What might you choose to do differently next
    time?

4. The last time you were involved in a major project,
    did you work with a team? If you were the leader,
    how did you determine who would be on the team?
    What would you look for in your next team? If you
    were a team member, how did you and your
    co-workers share in the task?

5. Is there a new dream or vision in your life that is just
    beginning to emerge? What kind of creative space do
    you need to be open to the "hovering" process?

The Leader as Intercessor

Chapter 8

Esther—The Leader Who Interceded *

The stories of female biblical leadership I have presented so far have all come from the stories of women from the ancient nation of Israel, a nation whose history is fraught with opposition and oppression. Taking up the torch long after the Exodus and the era of the Judges is our next leading lady, Esther. She stepped up to the challenge of leadership during a period hundreds of years after the flourishing monarchy of Israel.

Esther lived in the Persian capital of Susa during the reign of Xerxes, grandson of Cyrus the Great. Xerxes had deposed his first queen, Vashti, from the throne for what he considered to be insubordination for her unwillingness to be paraded in front of a banquet hall of drunken men at one of his feasts. Now the country was without a queen until Xerxes decided to choose a new one.

Although the king served as the official leader of the kingdom, the position of queen was important to the kingdom. She managed an entourage of servants, workers, and advisors, and, along with the king, represented the people at official state ceremonies and events. The queen typically, although not always, had access to the man in power and therefore might have the ability to influence the king in ways no other person could.

---

* *The account of Esther's leadership can be found in the Book of Esther.*

The process for choosing a new queen was prescribed and protracted. The king would commission his servants to round up beautiful women throughout the territory and bring them to the palace. For one full year the women would be sequestered in living quarters especially reserved for the king's harem. Each woman would be given daily luxurious spa treatments and prepared for her initial encounter with the king—a night of intimacy. Those who brought the most pleasure to the king would be advanced to round two. From this group the king would choose his new queen.

Being in the Right Place

Esther was a young Jewish woman whose parents had died and who had been raised by Mordecai, a male relative. Along with hundreds of other young women, she had been brought to the palace to be evaluated as a possible new queen. Mordecai, who worked in the palace, was able to maintain some contact with her through a network of servants and workers and urged her not to reveal her Jewish identity to members of the Persian court.

After a year of beauty treatments and preparations, Esther was selected above all the other women who were vying to be Queen of Persia. Some suggest it was Esther's beauty or her physical prowess that caught the king's attention. The only thing we know for certain is that the hand of God is evident in Esther's story as "she obtained grace and favor" in the king's sight (Esther 2:17, NKJV).

Yet it is not in Esther's official capacity as queen that we see her transformative leadership, but in the role she assumed on behalf of her people—the Jews who remained outside of their homeland, the Jews of the Diaspora.[1] In accepting the challenge to tell her people's story, Esther became an intercessory leader—a spokesperson and advocate for her people.

In order to appreciate the rise of Esther to this leadership, we must understand the circumstances that called her forth. A key player in this story is Haman, a man whom King Xerxes had appointed as vizier or top official in the Persian palace. An arrogant man, Haman had demanded that all the servants in the palace bow down and pay homage to him. When Mordecai refused, the other servants were resentful and reported his insubordination to Haman, attributing his refusal to his Jewish identity.

Haman was irate, but instead of seeking retribution against Mordecai alone, Haman set out to destroy Mordecai and all his people. Haman approached the king with an elaborately deceptive plan to destroy all the Jews in the Persian kingdom, arguing that they remained "unassimilated" or "segregated" in the kingdom and, as an ethnic group, they posed grave danger.[2]

Haman not only accused the Jews of disobeying Persian laws, he stereotyped them, attributing false traits to the entire group. He convinced the king that Mordecai's disrespect extended to the multitude of Persian Jews. To further assure the king's approval of his twisted plan, Haman offered to deposit ten thousand talents into the royal treasury, perhaps as a means of compensating the king for the tax revenue that would be lost once the Jews were exterminated.[3] The king approved Haman's plan and gave Haman his signet ring to seal the orders—an edict that could not be reversed, according to Persian custom.

The date of the mass genocide was set nearly a year in advance, and the edict was dispatched to all officials throughout the kingdom. The order was this: On the thirteenth day of the twelfth month the people of Persia were to kill all Jews—young old, male and female—and to take all their possessions.

Being Open to the Need

Mordecai eventually learned about Haman's genocidal plan, but there was nothing he could do to circumvent this scheme. Meanwhile, Esther was nestled safely inside the palace, oblivious to the happenings of the day. Mordecai had to conceive a way to alert her to the situation because he knew she might be the only one in a position to thwart this heinous plan.

To get Esther's attention, Mordecai tore his clothes and put on sackcloth and ashes—the garments of mourning—and proceeded to the middle of the city square where he wailed and cried aloud. He paraded through the streets and up to the king's gates, lamenting the condition of his people. (Mordecai was not alone in his grief, for Jewish people throughout the land had assumed the same posture of grieving: they wept, they fasted, they lay in sackcloth and ashes.)

When Esther's servants told her of Mordecai's unusual behavior, the queen was deeply distressed and confused over the cause and meaning of his actions. So she ordered one of her officials, Hatach, to go to the city square and find out what was going on. Mordecai told him about the death plan and gave him a copy of the decree to give to Esther. He then instructed Hatach to "urge her to go into the king's presence to beg for mercy and plead with him for her people" (Esther 4:8).

When Hatach explained the situation to Esther, she sent him back to Mordecai, presenting all reasons why she could not go into the king—primarily because she had not been summoned. For her to go on her own initiative might cause her own death. The king was a volatile man and might receive her . . . or he might not. One never knew.

Mordecai's return message raised (and perhaps pricked) her consciousness. He warned Esther against self-preservation, cautioning that if, in her efforts to save herself, deliverance for her people arose from another place, Esther's silence would not save her. Then Mordecai confronted her with these now timeless words that resonate in the spirit of every leader challenged to fight for justice and to work on behalf of others: ". . . and who knows but that you have come to the royal position for such a time as this?" (Esther 4:14).

Mordecai's next challenge points to an important condition for intercessory leadership: *The intercessor cannot truly tell another's story until she gets in touch with her own and sees the interconnections.* Mordecai charged Esther with reviewing her own life story, for though she was a Jew living incognito, her personal story, her very being, was inextricably linked to the story of all the Jews of the Diaspora. For Esther to remain silent would be to deny not only the story of her people but her own. The cultural and life narrative of Esther's people was deeply intertwined with the story of God and God's relationship with the Jewish people. By telling the story of her people, Esther would also be telling the story of God. As Lee Schlesinger, Professor of English at the State University of New York, puts it: "If you are going to tell the story of God, you are also telling the story of the people, and if you are going to tell the story of the people, then you are also telling the story of God."[4]

Esther could no longer remain silent. She knew she had to request justice for her people and bring honor to her God.

If you have ever put up a fight—determined to do things your own way or determined to stubbornly continue down a path that seemed perfectly logical—only to be awakened in your deepest senses to the reality of what you must do, then you know the sobering and humbling moment that Esther experienced when, with new resolve and conviction, she determined, "I will go to the king which is against the law, and if I perish, I perish" (Esther 4:16). At that moment, Esther assumed leadership for her people's relief. Her story changed from that of a passive beauty queen and royal ornament to an active agent of change. Her actions would forever shape her destiny and that of her people.

Esther's next move makes the second condition for intercessory leadership clear: *We cannot work on behalf of others without clarity of purpose.* Esther commanded Mordecai: "Go gather together all the Jews who are in Susa, and fast for me. Do not eat or drink for three days, neither night or day. I and my maids will fast as you do" (Esther 4:16). She put a plan in place that would open her to spiritual direction, for fasting has been an age-old discipline in seeking divine guidance and gaining clarity of purpose.

Understanding Go d's Timing

Esther had an important message to share and a critical story to tell, but she knew the full impact of the story could only be felt at the proper time. She could not blurt it out nor rush through her story. Esther understood this condition of leadership: *The intercessor operates within*

God's timeframe, not her own. It is a wise intercessor who discerns the seasons of events and waits for God's timing before she moves.

No doubt three days of fasting slowed Esther down and synchronized her to the cadence of heaven. Esther could not rush toward the king: She could not upset his sense of order or ego. God had to touch his heart first. So on the third day Esther put on her royal robes. She assumed the full regalia befitting of the mighty queen she had become and stepped just inside the inner court of the king's palace. There he sat, dressed in his robes of state, glittering with gold and precious stones—a formidable sight.[5] We are told the king's heart was softened at the sight of Esther, and he stretched out his scepter to welcome her into his presence.

Because coming into the king's presence without invitation was against the law, the king surely realized the importance of Esther's unannounced visit. Esther would not have interrupted the state of affairs for a simple familial matter! He, of course, wanted to know what had brought her to the palace, but sensing that is was not time to disclose her full request, Esther started with a pleasant invitation: "If it pleases the king, let the king together with Haman, come today to a banquet that I have prepared for him" (Esther 5:4).

The king accepted.

At Esther's "banquet of wine" (Esther 5:6, NKJV), the king inquired of her once again what it was she wanted. Again, Esther delayed. "If the king regards me with favor and if it pleases the king to grant my petition and fulfill my request, let the king and Haman come to the banquet I will prepare for them. Then I will answer the king's question" (Esther 5:8). The king agreed to join Esther with Haman again on the next day.

What a difference a day makes.

As Haman was leaving the banquet, he saw Mordecai sitting at the king's gate and became irate all over again. At home, Haman gathered his wife and friends to brag about his personal time spent with the king and queen, but the thought of Mordecai nagged at his pride and he could not fully enjoy his moment of glory. Sensing Haman's impatience for Mordecai's execution, his wife and friends gave him an idea that would expedite Mordecai's removal. They persuaded Haman to secure the king's permission the next morning to hang Mordecai on 50-cubit (75-feet) high gallows in the city square. He went to bed happy that his mortal enemy would finally be destroyed.

In the meantime—and there is always a meantime in God's plan—the king could not sleep. The "meantime" is a time of waiting, a time when we may think nothing is happening. It is often in the meantime of waiting that God stirs. In the meantime of this story, the king suffered from insomnia. He called for some bedtime reading, the books of the royal chronicles. The servant happened to read him an entry describing the uncovering of an assassination plot. This obscure but timely story jarred the king's memory: He recalled that, a few years earlier, Mordecai had uncovered an assassination plot devised by the royal doorkeepers against the king and had told Esther about this plot. The king's life had been spared and the doorkeepers executed. The king was pricked in his conscious. He wondered if he had he ever honored Mordecai for his heroic actions. The servant confirmed that he had not.

At that moment—perhaps by now it was daybreak—Haman entered into the outer court. In his consuming urgency to destroy Mordecai, he rushed to set an appointment with the king to share his latest scheme. When the king ordered Haman to come in, he asked Haman rather obliquely, "What shall be done for the man the king delights to honor?" (Esther 4:6).

In his arrogance Haman thought, 'Who would the king like to honor more than me?' and proceeded to articulate all of his own lavish desires for fame and visibility. The king was delighted. He commanded Mordecai to be brought to the palace immediately and instructed that all the lavish honors named by Haman be heaped upon Mordecai, the man who had saved the king's life.

In an ironic twist, Mordecai ended up receiving honor—the king's robe and a horseback ride through the city square—from the hand of Haman. After the parade, Haman was mortified, sulking to his wife and friends. No doubt he cheered up as he was whisked away for Queen Esther's second banquet.

Taking Action

To intervene means to step into a situation and alter its direction, its course, or its dynamics. There comes a place and time when the conditions are right and the intercessory leader must act. The time had come for Esther to change the course of her people's destiny.

Esther's intervention was timely and effective. It started with her entreaty to the king to save her people's lives, as well as her own life. From there Esther proceeded to tell the story of her people's plight to the king. Finally her intervention culminated with her plan for her people to defend themselves.

Esther had transformed from one who hid her identity to one who not only disclosed her true identity but identified with the plight of her people so much so that she interceded and intervened on their behalf. Though she was queen, she identified with the dispossessed, the threatened. She spoke courageously on behalf of the Jewish people, and on her own behalf, in terms that the king could readily grasp. This ability to speak across cultural and political boundaries points to another condition of intercessory leadership: *The intercessor must learn the language of her people and be able to tell their story in language to which the powers-that-be can relate.*

For every intercessory leader, there comes a time when she must confront the present realities and tell her truth. When challenged to reveal the culprit who had threatened her, it was time for Esther to confront her enemy: "The adversary and enemy is this wicked Haman!" (Esther 7:6, NKJV). In a supreme twist of irony, Haman was executed on the very gallows he had prepared for Mordecai.

Yet even though the people's story had been told and the enemy destroyed, the Jews were still in danger. The law of the Medes and Persians prevented the king's original order from being rescinded! So Esther had to devise a plan that would enable her people to survive the onslaught of destruction. This points to the ultimate goal of every intercessory leader: to prepare and equip people to speak for themselves, to fight for their own freedom.

Though the first decree could not be undone, the king gave Esther authority to write another decree that counteracted the first decree. Esther wrote a letter under the king's signature that "granted the Jews in every city the right to assemble and protect themselves" (Esther 8:11). For two days the Jews defended their lives, their families, and their possessions from those who sought to annihilate them.

The Power of the Intercessor

The close of the book of Esther recounts the institution of the Feast of Purim, the annual celebration commemorating the "time when the Jews got relief from their enemies" (Esther 9:22). It was through Esther's leadership that those days were "turned from sorrow to joy for them and from mourning to a holiday" (Esther 9:22).

Esther had been transformed from the orphan girl of the Diaspora to the influential Queen of Persia, from one to whom orders are given to one who gives orders. Her intercessory leadership provides us with a series of lessons about intercessory leadership that aims to improve the conditions and plight of other people:

The intercessory leader is strategically placed by the hand of God and becomes part of God's plan to shape the narrative of a people.

The intercessory leader steps up to the challenge when the time arises.

The intercessory leader comes to recognize the opportunities to intervene that transcend mere coincidence.

The intercessory leader has to speak and translate two languages and be conscious of multiple realities.

Ultimately, Esther's story reminds us of the power of empowerment. The intercessory leader must be able to communicate across the divide in order to empower people—the end result of helping people fight for themselves.

Reflection and Discussion Questions

1. Who can you think of who intercedes or fights for other people? How does she do this?

2. How do you respond to injustice when you see it? What vehicles do you use to raise awareness around issues of injustice? What lessons can you learn from Esther on interceding for people in need of your help?

3. Was there ever a time when you looked past your own safety for the benefit of others? What was the outcome?

4. Have you ever experienced a "meantime," waiting on God's timing? How did you feel during this time? What wisdom did you gain in the "meantime"?

5. Think of situations in which, like Esther, you consciously waited for the right moment to make a request. What impact did waiting have on the result?

Chapter 9

The Leader as Intercessor

Intercession is a pivotal theological concept—one that is woven throughout biblical history. Sometimes intercession refers to the act of going between two contesting parties with the view toward mediation and reconciliation. At other times, intercession means entreaty on behalf of another. Intercession can also imply accompanying another person to provide support and strength.

God has always provided humanity with an intercessor—one who bridges the gap between the human and the Divine. The Bible is filled with examples of women and men who served as intercessors for other people, connecting human to human, and humans to God. Abraham, Joseph, Moses, Ruth, Esther, and Isaiah each in their own way interceded for God's people. Job, in his pain and suffering, cried out for an intercessor. Feeling estranged from God, he wondered if a mediator existed who could identify with his story and intercede with God on his behalf to end his pain and suffering (Job 9:33). Job's cry was a call for the seemingly impossible: someone who could fully identify with God and with humanity at the same time. Yet his plight prophetically set the stage for the coming of the ultimate intercessor—Jesus Christ, who lives to make perpetual intercession for us (Hebrews 7:25). The New Testament describes the Holy Spirit as our *paracletos*—one who walks along side another to comfort and console, accompanying us on our spiritual journeys, interceding for us in prayer (Romans 8:26). Many churches and denominations have developed a vibrant and powerful ministry of prayer intercessors who "stand in the gap" (Ezekiel 22:30) for people, neighborhoods, and entire countries. All of these intercessors, both ancient and contemporary, may be called gap-dwellers, for they stand in the gap between the beseecher and the beseeched.

Some leaders are called specifically to stand in the gap—the space between contesting parties, between policymakers and poor people, between powerbrokers and the disempowered—to bring about transformation or change. These intercessors work in the space between extremes—between poverty and wealth, between despair and hope. This is not a comfortable space, and they live with the tension of the contradictions and paradoxes of life. While intercessory leaders are aware that they have access to information, resources, and power that others do not, the core gifts of the intercessor are her willingness to tell the story of others and her ability to tell the story in a way that will move the heart of the one in power. The ultimate goal of the intercessory leader is to enable those with no voice to gain a voice.

Called into the Gap

Reverend Willie Tapplin Barrow is an intercessory leader who has been called into the gap time and again to help the portions of humanity left on the fringes of power. Rev. Barrow is the chair of the board of the Rainbow/PUSH Coalition, an organization devoted to fighting for social, racial, and economic justice for people of diverse ethnic, religious, economic, and political backgrounds.

Known as "a voice of the community," Rev. Barrow has dedicated her life to speaking for those who cannot speak for themselves.[1] In the 1960s she was one of three founding members of the first national staff of Operation Breadbasket, one of the initiatives launched by Dr. Martin Luther King, Jr. to fight hunger and poverty. A trained welder, Rev. Barrow has been a leader in the labor movement, advocating fair wages and working conditions. Today Rev. Barrow maintains an active speaking schedule, raising awareness on issues relevant to families, health, and women.

Rev. Barrow affirms that she was called by God to do what she does and believes that her calling into leadership was a gift from God, evident even at a young age. She tells the story of her first demonstration for equality against a segregated rural school system that did not provide the black children of the town with school buses, as it did for white students. Ten-year-old Willie and her school friends had to walk the long, dusty trek to school. Even though the bus passed right by them on its way to and from the school, the driver was not permitted to stop for them because of their color.

The black students often complained about their plight—"Why do we have to walk to school?"—but their complaints fell on deaf ears. One day, as she and her fellow schoolmates were walking to school, Willie looked back and saw the bus approaching. She decided *that* day she was going to do something about it. She proclaimed to the group, "I'm tired of walking. I'm going to jump on that bus. Why should we have to walk?" As the bus slowly drew near, Willie's schoolmates cheered her on. She was taking action on behalf of all of them.

In those days, the buses had open cabs in back, so as this bus slowly passed, Willie ran behind and jumped on. For about a half mile she created quite a stir on the bus, and the driver finally stopped to see what was going on. Amid his regular riders he found little Willie being bombarded by a mixture of taunts and jeers—and some supportive words.

It happened that Willie was the daughter of one of the prominent black pastors in the town, so the bus driver readily recognized her. "You have to go. We're going to have to tell your father," the driver told her. Willie got off that bus, little knowing that her active resistance would create a stir in her town, starting people, black and white, to talk about "what Reverend Tapplin's daughter did." The incident started people talking about the issues, and within a few years the school system got a black superintendent. Rev. Barrow attributes that hire to the ripple effect of her actions. Young Willie was thrust into the gap because she was moved to respond to unjust conditions. Her actions confirm that even the smallest act of resistance against injustice can yield monumental results.

Today, as a minister and community advocate, Rev. Barrow receives hundreds of telephone calls each week from people in need of help. These calls serve as a barometer for her, registering the economic, social, and relational plights people are facing. She relates the calls to current issues, places a human story behind the statistics, and presents the issues to political and community leaders. Although Rev. Barrow touches government leaders, social agencies, and businesses, she never loses her clarity of purpose—to help people who do not have the access, and to educate and inform the powers that be. She knows that it is critical to listen and understand what people are facing.

For only when the intercessory leader can identify with the people for whom she advocates will she be able to adequately speak for them and tell their story.

Listening to the People

Sometimes women are in positions to influence other people's lives even though they do not hold the formal title of "leader." Yet because of what they do—moving people toward collective goals of transformation—they demonstrate the skills of leadership and act as intercessory leaders.

Prya* is one such person. Under older, more traditional definitions of leadership, Prya would not be considered a leader. Yet because of the work she does as a researcher for a community development foundation, she is a powerful intercessory leader for her people.

Prya goes out into the community to talk to people to determine what their needs are, collecting vital information that will ultimately affect and help to transform their lives.

For her first project, Prya was assigned to a "welfare to work" program. Even though she had more formal education than the women she visited, she never saw herself, or carried herself, as the "all knowing" expert coming in to push new programs. Instead, she listened closely to what the women were saying. She listened to their stories, their hopes, and their fears. And she learned a lot from the women of the community.

Too often people in power make decisions for people not in power—at least that is how it feels to the people not in power. The most effective leaders are those

I have used a pseudonym to tell the story of this intercessory leader. Many intercessory leaders are nameless; often times they work behind the scenes to bring about change in the forefront.

who listen well, who can tap into the aspirations and needs of people to understand the true transformative goal. Leaders who do not listen to the people with whom or for whom they work too easily fall into the trap of pushing their own purposes, sometimes at the expense of the purposes and needs of others. The intercessory leader listens carefully and understands the importance of accurately representing the peoples' position.

Making the Connection

The intercessory leader has to connect with people so that she can truly work on their behalf. Prya readily admits, "I don't see myself as the expert or the only one who has access to knowledge. I realize that the people on whose behalf I work are not much different than I am."

On the surface Prya appears to be totally different from her clients. She was raised in an affluent family and attended prestigious schools. Yet she recalls a time when she was in trouble and could not get the resources she needed. She had been harassed by a stalker and was eventually brutally attacked. She recalls feeling helpless because she had not been able to get the authorities to understand the immediacy of her danger until it was too late. Traumatized and bruised, she could not seem to find anyone who understood or who could relate to her fear and her anger. She felt she could not talk to her family, and her friends seemed alienated from her.

Prya recalls, "I had to learn a whole new way of going about life. I know what it feels like not to be able to get the help you need simply because you can't seem to talk to those who have the help. Many of the women with whom I talk in the community just haven't known how to get the resources they need."

Like Rev. Barrow, a deep sense of calling drives Prya. She believes her personal experience of trauma allows her to connect with the pain and need of the people she hopes to help. From that place of identification, God can use her to work for change in the community to better the lives of the women with whom she works.

Making the Translation

From the very first time she conducted an assessment, Prya recognized that she served in an advocacy role. She knew that, after she heard a woman's story, it was her responsibility to tell that story to decision makers and policy makers who could make a difference. She wanted to be careful to honor each woman's story, yet she realized that the women in the communities where she had been assigned spoke a different language than the policy makers. She saw her job as a translator between the group of women who did not have access to power and the group of policy makers who held the power.

One group spoke the poignant language of their experiences. The other group talked in statistics and dollars. The women spoke of their concerns about leaving their children with no one to watch them while they went off to work. Policy makers talked about shrinking the welfare rolls. The women talked about their concerns for making the long commute to the suburbs that took away even more family time. They wondered how they would fit into their new jobs, how the other workers would view them. And they talked about wanting to work and to provide their children with life that was better than theirs. As Prya listened to their concerns, she heard their underlying fear. These women were about to step into something new and were fearful of the unknown.

Here's how Prya describes her intercessory role of translator:

> I take what people tell me and retell it in another form or repackage it so as to help them get results to work toward some end. I gather data from people. I get to see their perspective. I synthesize. I know frameworks and models into which to translate what they tell me. I can take what these people tell me, translate it into another way of saying it, and present to policy makers so as to meet some need for this group.

So it will be with every leader who "stands in the gap" for someone else. She must be able to speak the language of the parties on either side of the divide, and she must be able to make the translation for both parties.

Working to Help People Gain Their Own Voice

An intercessory leader's role goes another step beyond speaking for those who have little or no voice; she also works to help people gain their *own* voice.

A few years back I received a call from Rev. Barrow concerning a cause she was called to assist. At that time, many of the public housing projects run by the city of Chicago were about to be placed into the hands of private landlords and property managers. A tenant, fondly known as "the mother of the CHA [Chicago Housing Authority]" had called one of the local community leaders who helped people in public housing residences organize the tenants. Together, these two women had formed the Local Action Council and had called Rev. Barrow for support.

Ever mindful of the "community of families" that existed within those housing developments, Rev. Barrow was concerned that new property managers would not care about the people who made those tenements home. She firmly believed that the residents of these housing projects needed to participate in selecting the new property managers, and she had advocated with CHA executives for tenant inclusion in the selection process. Because Rev. Barrow had access to CHA executives in ways that the tenants did not, she brought the issue of tenant inclusion to the executives in ways that made sense to them. Ultimately, they agreed to allow for citizen participation in the property management selection process.

They began their work by scheduling a meeting with the residents to clarify the issues and give them space to talk about their concerns and needs. Now that the tenants were about to be included in the process, they needed to be trained on how to best participate. I was honored to be called in as a resource. Rev. Barrow provided transportation for the citizens to the Rainbow/PUSH Coalition headquarters, and together we developed and implemented a training program.

Our first focus was on the residents who would serve on citizen boards that would eventually participate in the selection process for property managers. We equipped them with basic interviewing skills by holding a series of mock interviews with "potential landlords." This training gave them experience in assessing the qualities they needed to look for in a new landlord. The people left these training sessions excited that they would have input into major decisions that affected their live. They felt prepared to participate in a decision-making process that would have a profound and positive affect on their future. Most important, they knew their voice would be heard, and they felt empowered to affect the outcome.

Throughout this process, Rev. Barrow saw her role as having a double thrust: to bring the issues to the attention of the appropriate political leaders, and to bring trainers and other resources in to assist the residents. As an intercessory leader, Rev. Barrow not only fought on behalf of those who could not fight for themselves, but she also helped empower them so that they could join the fight on their own terms.

Placed to Intercede

Too often people in positions of authority do not see or understand the plight of people who do not have access to these decision-makers.

Too often people in positions of power do not understand the sense of futility experienced by people who see themselves as victims.

Too often processes are unjust and systematically leave out entire groups of people for unjust reasons.

Leaders such as Rev. Willie Bowman and Prya remind us of the pivotal roles that intercessory leaders play in working on behalf of others unable to work on their own behalf. Intercessory leaders provide another perspective, one that is often the opposite of the empowered view. They mediate and persuade, educate and influence, train and equip. Intercessory leaders change policies that change people's lives.

Some of you have been placed in the boardroom and will affect policy for those in the mailroom. Some of you are being called to work as advocates for women, children, and families who need help.

You are where you are for a reason; perhaps it is to serve as an intercessory leader for some person or group who does not have the same access you do.

Perhaps you are in a position to challenge an oppressive process in your community. Perhaps you have been called to your realm of influence for such a time as this.

Consider where you are being called to intercede. Stay prayerful about your role and the people for whom and the causes for which you intercede.

Reflection and Discussion Questions

1. Describe a leader you have known who acted as an intercessor. What were the causes for which she stood in the gap? In what ways did she advocate for these causes? How did she get others to understand the issues?

2. What kind of listener are you? Have you ever found yourself "translating" the words of one person, perhaps for a child, a family member, or a co-worker, so another could understand? How were you able to help the two parties find some common ground?

3. What are some key issues about which you feel passionately? In what ways do you keep abreast of these issues? Can you identify an area where your voice or action might be influential?

4. How might information that you possess help someone else? How might you share this information? What support would help you share this information with others?

5. Where in your life might you be in a position to challenge oppressive pressures or systems? Where do you have access that others have not? How might you use your access to help better the lives or conditions of other people?

Chapter 10

From Image to Impact

Maria had lived in one community all of her life. Her parents and parents' parents had also lived there. She had worked in her family's business, spent lots of time with her relatives, and had enjoyed life in her idyllic island community surrounded by family and friends.

But she had noticed the neighboring communities beginning to change. The country charm was being replaced by large-scale resort development. Local people who had owned and lived on the land for generations were now losing their land. In the place of simple farms and farmer's markets, massive island resorts were being developed. Tourists flocked to these islands, and gated communities were built on land that once belonged to native people. Land that was once considered to be communal property belonging to all the people was now blocked off, to be enjoyed only by the newest residents.

In her own neighborhood Maria was also beginning to see signs of deterioration. The younger people were going away to college and not returning. They were finding well-paying jobs in larger cities. The older members of the community found it more difficult to pay the taxes to maintain their property, and some were beginning to think it would be easier to sell the property to a developer and move away, as their children had done.

Yet Maria yearned to maintain the integrity of the island, for it was a place rich in heritage and culture. One day she saw a notice in her church bulletin announcing the formation of a Community Leadership School whose programs would train local citizens to band together to effect change in their community. The founders of the school, sponsored by the local Community Action Center, believed that training community leaders was the key for creating and working toward a positive future.

Maria wondered whether or not she should join the school, for she had never seen herself as a leader. She considered herself just an "ordinary, everyday person." But she deeply desired to help turn her community around and prevent it from becoming an island playground for the rich and famous, as had neighboring islands.

The training attracted a broad variety of people—people concerned about maintaining the culture of the island, environmentalists wanting to preserve the island ecosystem, plus a few local politicians, business people, church members, school teachers, and retired senior citizens—all in all, a number of "ordinary" people like Maria. The training lasted for six months, and the members learned a variety of skills and methods for developing a brighter future for their community—a future that honored the cultural heritage of the past, optimized the environmental riches of the present, and created opportunities for economic development for the future.

I talked with Maria shortly after she had completed the leadership training program, and she told me, "Before this school, I never saw myself as a leader. I now know that I can lead and make a difference in my community. I have joined with other leaders and have learned methods for developing a shared vision for our community, analyzing where we currently are, developing strategies, and creating new policies to help us realize that vision."

The school had given Maria a new image of leadership. Before, she had thought only elected officials were leaders of the community. She had believed only certain people could lead, only a select few had influence. She now had a new vision of what it meant to be a leader. She had found a place where she could join with others in leading the community toward a hopeful future. She had seen that she had abilities that could make a difference. And she was now willing and ready to launch an effort to make an impact on her community.

That is really the core goal of this book: to help you see yourself as a leader. I hope the images of the women of the Bible, and the stories of the contemporary women who walk in their footsteps, have helped you see your potential and what you can become. I hope your thinking about what it means to be a leader, what it takes to lead, and who can lead has been challenged.

Like Maria, many of you reading this book may never have seen yourself as a leader. I have attempted to put leadership in a new light, to show that "leading ladies" are ordinary women who face real challenges and work to transform the conditions of the people around them.

Each leading lady from the Bible did just that —made an impact for good in the situations in which they had been placed. These women went about doing good in ways that were distinctive of female leadership. Each contemporary leading lady was an ordinary, everyday woman who made herself available to be used by God to make impact on the lives of others.

Some of you may have identified more readily with one particular image of leadership than another. This may suggest the style of leadership that is your primary style. You may be gifted at seeing the possibilities in people and be feeling called to midwife others to their full potential. You may have grasped a vision and be feeling called to choreograph the concept so that others can dance that vision. You may be called to weave together plans and teams that help others realize their vision. You may be called to speak your vision of justice on behalf of those who have been silenced.

Others of you may have identified with many, if not all, of the images. For you, the key will be to determine when to use a given style, to assess which circumstances call forth midwifery, choreographing, weaving, or interceding.

I hope you will use the following summaries to help you compare each of the leadership qualities and identify, hone, and use your particular God-given gifts.

Identifying Your Leadership Image

The Leader as MIDWIFE tends to:
- lead one person at a time
- focus in on and develop one-on-one relationships
- encourage another person to develop her or his untapped potential
- motivate another person to be and do more than she thought she could on her own
- accompany another person through a developmental or growth process
- provide care, nourishment, and support through difficult times
- prod people to push through pain

The Leader as CHOREOGRAPHER tends to:
- move groups of people to own a vision
- provoke people to see old things in new ways.
- develop and hone the skills of other people
- motivate individuals to overcome hurdles
- teach people new steps or creative ways of doing things
- express ideas and truth to people in dramatic ways
- bring people together for a collective endeavor

The Leader as WEAVER tends to:
- help clarify their own or another person's vision
- develop a strategic process to bring the vision to life
- seek a team of people to carry out the strategic plan
- set strategic goals with a team
- help people believe in the vision and in themselves
- identify and delegate tasks needed to achieve the goal
- determine a leadership pattern that is appropriate to her situation, tasks, and people.

The Leader as INTERCESSOR tends to:
- name conditions in need of change
- identify with the people affected by those conditions
- identify resources needed for change
- advocate for those affected by conditions in need of change
- start with people whose skills and abilities have been overlooked, mislabeled or not valued
- push systems to change
- equip people to advocate for themselves

A New Generation of Leaders

I began this book by describing my Granny, my first pastor. In many ways Granny was part midwife, part choreographer, part weaver, and part intercessor.

As a midwife, Granny birthed my mother and her generation of church leaders. She also helped to create the conditions under which my generation came into leadership in the church.

Granny loved to sing and was often called upon during the district church services to sing her songs. As she sang a story of God's power and presence in their lives, she would sing herself and the congregation "happy." They would dance and shout, and as a choreographer, Granny would lead the dancing. They celebrated God's power in their lives, releasing the pain and frustration of the day and refocusing on God.

As weaver, Granny spun a tight-knit clan of six daughters and three sons. She instilled within her children the importance of family unity and connection. To this day, the tapestry of four generations of close-knit cousins and aunts and uncles is a tribute to my grandmother's tender weaving of strong relationships within the extended church family.

I spent a lot of time with Granny when I was young. I remember Saturday evenings sprawled out atop her bed, watching television with her. I now realize the television was more to keep me company because, as Granny lay across the bed studying her Bible, I could see her eyes closed and mouth moving. Every now and then I would hear words come out of her mouth, such as, "Lord, keep Tommy, wherever he is." She would be praying for one of her rambunctious grandsons. At other times, she would say someone else's name and ask God for something on their behalf. My Granny was praying for us, her grand-children, as well as for many other people. Granny was the first intercessor I knew long before I understood what an intercessor was. She prayed for us. She worked on our be-half. My generation of leaders and I are the answers to some of those prayers.

May you lead, like my Granny, in the tradition of Puah and Shiphrah, Miriam, Deborah, and Esther. May you discover your own leadership gift as midwife, choreographer, weaver, or intercessor. And may you go forth as the leading lady you were destined to be.

Reflection and Discussion Questions

1. What common themes do you see in the four leadership images? What lessons can you draw from these characteristics for your own leadership?

2. Of all the leadership images offered in this book, which one(s) more closely resonate with you? What distinctive qualities about this leadership image match your personality style?

3. In what ways can clarifying your style help you to be more effective as a leader?

4. What situations seem to be calling for your leadership? How do you feel about this?

Endnotes

INTRODUCTION

1. Dr. Vashti McKenzie is one of the first writers to include women of the biblical text in the leadership discourse. See Vashti McKenzie, *Not Without a Struggle*, especially pages 73-76.

2. There are a number of female leaders of antiquity, too many obviously for this one book. Dr. McKenzie uses a framework developed by Robert Dale to describe the leadership of a number of female "biblical role models" (*Not Without a Struggle*, p. 73). McKenzie's analysis is helpful in providing us with a leadership lens to view the stories of women in the Bible. In doing so, she shows the applicability of a leadership model for women and in many ways legitimates our calling these women of antiquity leaders. In this book, my aim is to expand on McKenzie's work by examining the women leaders of the past more closely.

3. See Drorah O'Donnell Setel's chapter "Exodus" in *The Women's Bible Commentary*. Setel identifies Puah and Shiphrah as two of "numerous women who play significant, although unelaborated roles in the events described in" Exodus. Setel continues to suggest that these women's "stories may be the remnants of a larger cycle that recorded women's as well as men's involvement in the leadership of the people. The texts we do have imply that to the extent women provided guidance they acted either in rebellion (1:17), without explicit authority (4:25), or within a separate female sphere (15:20-21)" (*The Women's Bible Commentary*, p. 29).

4. Setel's observations in *The Women's Bible Commentary* about female leadership in the Exodus narrative also support my inclusion of the sister of Moses, Miriam the Prophetess, in my analysis of biblical women's leadership.

5. The Judge was both an administrative, political, and a military leader who ruled specific regions during biblical times. Deborah's

leadership is noted as unique for her day not only because she was the only woman among the twelve Judges but also because she was said to be judging even before she was sent into battle.

6. James MacGregor Burns (*Leadership*, 1978) used the term "transformational" or "transforming leadership," and Bennis and Nanus (*Leaders*, 1997) used the term "transformative leadership." The framework of transformative leadership developed in this book builds upon both definitions and is taken from the biblical principle of transformation found in key scriptures such as Romans 12:1-2. The spiritual principle of transformation calls for a renewal of mind or perspective that does not conform to the established or prevailing perspective of the society. The idea that God calls women and men from all walks of life to lead according to God's plan and purposes does not conform to the traditional and prevailing notion of leadership popularized and reproduced in our culture.

CHAPTER 1: Women Have Always Led

1. See pages 91-93 of Cheryl Townsend Gilkes, "The Politics of 'Silence': Dual-sex Political Systems and Women's Traditions of Conflict in African-American Religion" for an account of the church mothers in African American religious traditions.

2. See Patricia Hayes Andrews, "Sex and Gender Differences in Group Communication: Impact on the Facilitation Process," and W.F. Owen, "Rhetorical Themes of Emergent Leaders."

3. See Sally Helgesen, *The Female Advantage: Women's Ways of Leadership*.

4. Lisa Anderson, "Why Can't a Woman Run For President Today?" *Chicago Tribune* 10/31/99.

5. Private conversations with a long-time Lucent manager.

6. "50 Most Powerful Women," http://www.fortune.com/fortune/mostpowerful/1.html.

CHAPTER 2: Puah and Shiprah

1. William Sears and Martha Sears, *The Birth Book*.

2. According to Frederick Coplestone in *A History of Philosophy*, Phaenarete, the mother of Socrates, is said to have been a midwife (p. 96). Additionally, Martha Ballard a rural eighteenth-century midwife from Maine is featured on the DoHistory.org website.

3. Gloria Naylor, *Mama Day*.

4. See Linda Holmes chapter in *The Black Woman's Health Book,* pp. 98-106.

5. See Herbert Lockyer, *All the Women of the Bible,* p. 126. Some scholars suggest the midwives names are of Semitic origin; Puah, meaning "shining one," and Shiphrah, meaning "beauty." Most agree that they were "two among many" midwives to serve the Hebrew women and their courageous act of resistance made them women of influence. See Meyers, *Women in Scripture,* pp. 137-138, for a critical discussion on Puah and Shiphrah.

6. *Strong's Exhaustive Concordance,* entry #3372.

7. See Jack Hayford's *Electronic Spirit-Filled Life Application Bible,* p. 85.

CHAPTER 3: The Leader as Midwife

1. Bishop Carlton Pearson, "Mother Sherman Story," *Live at Azusa 2,* Warner Alliance CD, 1997.

CHAPTER 4: Miriam

1. See Lerone Bennett, *Before the Mayflower.*

CHAPTER 5: The Leader as Choreographer

1. *Nelson's New Illustrated Bible Dictionary.*

2. *International Encyclopedia of Dance, Vol. 1,* p. 448.

3. *International Encyclopedia of Dance, Vol. 1,* p. 488.

4. *International Encyclopedia of Dance, Vol. 1,* p. 488

5. Bridget Mary Meehan, *Praying with Visionary Women.*

6. Interview with Father Michael Pfleger, civil rights activist and parish priest of the Faith Community of St. Sabina, Chicago, IL.

7. Interview with Father Pfleger.

8. Interview with Father Pfleger.

9. See chapter 14, "She Made the Bishops Dance," by Marie Augusta Neal in *Thea Bowman: Handing on Her Own Legacy.*

10. *Sr. Thea: Her Own Story, A Video Autobiography.* Oblate Media and Communication, 1991.

11. *Sr. Thea: Her Own Story, A Video Autobiography.*

12. *Sr. Thea: Her Own Story, A Video Autobiography.*

CHAPTER 6: Deborah

1. See *The Women's Bible Commentary*, p. 69.

2. For an in-depth discussion of Deborah's strategy, see *Nelson's New Illustrated Bible Manners and Customs*.

CHAPTER 7: The Leader as Weaver

1. See the *Dictionary of Art* for comprehensive and insightful accounts of the weaving traditions of various cultures.

2. Weavers produce fabric by interlacing two sets of yarn (one set of yarn constitutes the length of the fabric and the other set makes the width) so that they cross each other. The lengthwise yarns are called warp and the cross-wise yarns are called weft or filling. See the *Dictionary of Art, Vol. 34*, p. 542 for a detailed description of weaving.

3. See Hayford's *Electronic Spirit-Filled Life Bible*.

CHAPTER 8: Esther

1. Esther was part of the Jewish Diaspora. The period of the exile started as early as 745 B.C.E. when the Hebrews were deported from their homeland and colonized by the military powers of Assyria and Babylon. In 539 B.C.E. Babylon was conquered by Persia, whose King Cyrus the Great issued a decree allowing the Jews to return to their homeland and to rebuild their Temple. Many Jews remained in Babylon or migrated to other regions in the Persian kingdom. This group of Jews who remained outside of Palestine became known as the Jewish Diaspora. See *Harper's Bible Dictionary*, p 178.

2. See Fox's *Character and Ideology in the Book of Esther*, pp. 46-49, for an expanded translation of Esther 3:7.

3. See Fox's *Character and Ideology in the Book of Esther*, pp. 51-52, for support of this argument.

4. Quoted in Martha C. Bartholomew, *Tellers of Story—Keepers of Dream*, p. 11.

5. A vivid account of the queen's encounter with the king is given in *The Jerusalem Bible*.

CHAPTER 9: The Leader as Intercessor

1. Rainbow/PUSH's website is www.rainbowpush.org.

Bibliography

Andrews, Patricia Hayes. "Sex and Gender Differences in Group Communication: Impact on the Facilitation Process." *Small Group Research*, 1992:23 (pp 74-94).

Bartholomew, Martha C. *Tellers of the Story—Keepers of Dream*. Bristol, IN: Wyndham Hall Press, 1998.

Bennett, Lerone, Jr. *Before the Mayflower: A History of Black America* (Sixth Ed.). Chicago: Johnson Publishing Company, 1987.

Bennis, Warren and Burt Nanus. *Leaders: Strategies for Taking Charge* (Second Edition). New York: Harper & Row, 1997.

Burns, James MacGregor. *Leadership*. New York: Harper & Row, 1978.

Coplestone, Frederick, S. J. *A History of Philosophy, Vols. I, II, III*. New York: Image Books/Doubleday, 1985.

Dictionary of Art, Vol. 34. Edited by Jane Turner. New York: Grove Dictionaries, Inc., 1996.

Dictionary of Biblical Imagery. Edited by Leland Ryken, James C. Whilhoit, and Tremper Longman III. Downer's Grove, IL: InterVarsity Press, 1998.

Eisenberg, Arlene, Heidi E. Murkoff, and Sandee E. Hathaway. *What to Expect When You're Expecting*. New York: Workman Publishing, 1996.

Fox, Michael V. *Character and Ideology in the Book of Esther*. Columbia: University of South Carolina Press, 1991.

Gibson, James E, *Healing Wisdom from the Bible: Spiritual Guidance, Inspiration, and Comfort for Everyday Life*. Emmaus, PA: The Good Spirit Press, 1989.

Gilkes, Cheryl Townsend. "The Politics of 'Silence': Dual-Sex Political Systems and Women's Traditions of Conflict in African-American Religion." In *African-American Christianity: Essays in History*, edited by Paul E. Johnson, pp. 80-110. Berkeley: University of California Press, 1994.

Harper's Bible Dictionary. Edited by Madeleine S. and J. Lane Miller. New York: Harper & Row, 1973.

Hayford, Jack, ed. *Electronic Spirit-Filled Life Bible*. Nashville: Thomas Nelson Publishers, 1998.

Helgesen, Sally. *The Female Advantage: Women's Ways of Leadership*. New York: Doubleday, 1990.

Holmes, Linda Janet. "Thank You Jesus to Myself: The Life of a Traditional Black Midwife. In *The Black Women's Health Book: Speaking for Ourselves* (Revised Edition), edited by Evelyn C. White, pp. 98-106. Seattle: Seal Press, 1994.

Howard, David M. Jr. *An Introduction to the Old Testament Historical Books*. Chicago: Moody Press, 1993.

International Encyclopedia of Dance , Vol. 1. "Dance in the Bible." Edited by Selma Jeanne Cohen. New York: Oxford University Press, 1998. (p. 448)

Lockyer, Herbert. *All the Women of the Bible*. Grand Rapids: Zondervan, n.d.

McKenzie, Vashti. *Not Without a Struggle: Leadership Development for African American Women in Ministry*. Cleveland, OH: United Church Press, 1996.

Meehan, Bridget Mary. *Praying with Visionary Women*. Franklin, WI: Sheed & Ward, 1999.

Naylor, Gloria. *Mama Day*. New York: Vintage Books, 1988.

Meyers, Carol (General Editor). *Women in Scripture: A Dictionary of Named and Unnamed Women in the Hebrew Bible, the Apocryphal/Deuterocanonical Books and the New Testament*. New York: Houghton Mifflin Company, 2000.

Neal, Marie Augusta. "She Made the Bishops Dance." In *Thea Bowman: Handing on Her Legacy*, edited by Christian Koontz, R.S.M. (pp. 54-57). Kansas City, MO: Sheed & Ward, 1991.

Nelson's New Illustrated Bible Manners and Customs. Edited by Ronald F. Youngblood. Nashville: Thomas Nelson Publishers, 1999.

Owen, W.F. "Rhetorical Themes of Emergent Leaders." *Small Group Behavior*, 1986:17 (pp. 475-486).

Sears, William, and Martha Sears. *The Birth Book*. Boston: Little, Brown and Company, 1994.

Setel, Drorah O'Donnell. "Exodus." In *The Women's Bible Commentary*, edited by Carol A. Newsome and Sharon H. Ringe (pp. 26-35). Louisville, KY: Westminster/John Knox Press, 1992.

Strong, James. *Strong's Exhaustive Concordance of the Bible*. Nashville: Abingdon, 1980.

Women's Bible Commentary, The. Edited by Carol A. Newsome and Sharon H. Ringe. Louisville, KY: Westminster/John Knox Press, 1992.

About the Author

JEANNE PORTER has dedicated her research and teaching to leadership, especially as it relates to women, churches, and communities of color. She is an Associate Professor of Communication Arts at North Park University and teaches "Leadership and Team Development" in the African American Leadership Partnership Program (AALP) at McCormick Theological Seminary in Chicago. As an associate minister at the Apostolic Church of God in Chicago and a popular workshop leader and conference speaker, she also can be heard on Gospel Radio 1390/WGCI AM in Chicago.

Dr. Porter holds a bachelor's and a master of science degree from Ohio State University in Columbus, and a Ph.D. in Communication from Ohio University in Athens. In addition, she has completed theological studies at United Theological Seminary in Dayton, Ohio. Dr. Porter is also the founder and president of TransPorter Communication, a ministry-based consulting company that provides leadership development and communication training for churches, corporations, and community organizations.

If you would like to schedule a retreat or seminar for your organization, or if you would like to share, for a future book, a story of a "leading lady," and how your leading lady fits one of the images of leadership shared in this book, please contact Dr. Porter at:

TransPorter Communication LLC
P.O. Box 8028
Chicago, IL 60680-8028
www.TransporterCommunication.com

Spiritual Classics that Call to the Deep Heart's Core

⚬ð *from Innisfree Press* ∞

Just a Sister Away

A Womanist Vision of Relationships in the Bible

By Renita Weems

For women hungry for stories of biblical women they can recognize and want to connect with their biblical sisters.

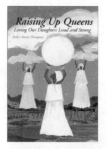

Raising Up Queens

Loving Our Daughters Loud and Strong

By Esther Davis-Thompson

Reflections of deep hope and encouragement for raising daughters to "sing their most real songs."

I Asked for Intimacy

Stories of Blessings, Betrayals, and Birthings

By Renita Weems

A poignant book of reflective essays that explore the issues that complicate our most significant relationships.

MotherLove

Reinventing a Good and Blessed Future for Our Children

By Esther Davis-Thompson

Inspiring, timely meditations on self-care, healing, love, and prayer with quotations from visionary women.

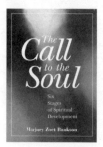

The Call to the Soul

Six Stages of Spiritual Development

By Marjory Zoet Bankson

A six-stage "soulwork cycle" to help seek and understand God's calling in life's transitions.

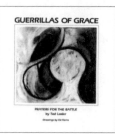

Guerrillas of Grace

Prayers for the Battle

By Ted Loder

Prayers that will feed your mind, lighten your heart, and dare your spirit. A best-seller for over 16 years!

Call for our free catalog
1-800-367-5872.

Innisfree Press books are available in your local bookstore.

Innisfree
Press, Inc.

A call to the deep heart's core

Visit our web site at
www.InnisfreePress.com.

Innisfree Press, Inc.
136 Roumfort Road
Philadelphia, PA 19119-1632